# James Garfield: The Life and Legacy of the Second President to Be Assassinated

**By Charles River Editors**

# About Charles River Editors

**Charles River Editors** provides superior editing and original writing services across the digital publishing industry, with the expertise to create digital content for publishers across a vast range of subject matter. In addition to providing original digital content for third party publishers, we also republish civilization's greatest literary works, bringing them to new generations of readers via ebooks.

Sign up here to receive updates about free books as we publish them, and visit Our Kindle Author Page to browse today's free promotions and our most recently published Kindle titles.

# Introduction

**The official White House portrait of Garfield**

"I never meet a ragged boy in the street without feeling that i may owe him a salute, for I know not what possibilities may be buttoned up under his coat." – James Garfield

He was the only sitting member of the House of Representatives elected President to date, but he served only about half a year in the office. He was the second president in less than 20 years felled by an assassin's bullet. Yet James A. Garfield, a man little known outside his own party before his "dark-horse" nomination by the Republican Party in 1880, was significant in a number of ways. Garfield's short term marked the first entrance of a "reformist" strain into the presidency that sought to root out corruption and political favoritism in government. Much of what we know as the modern federal bureaucracy has its roots in Garfield's advocacy of a professional civil service to fill most positions in the government, rather than filling those positions through political patronage, the "spoils system" that went back to the administration of Andrew Jackson. He did not live to see his proposed reforms enshrined in law, but Garfield's contribution to the history of the United States should not be underestimated.

In 1880, Garfield ran as a Republican for president, and one of his supporters was a man named Charles Guiteau, who wrote and circulated a speech called "Garfield vs. Hancock" that aimed to rally support for the Republican candidate. Though few knew it, Guiteau's family had already deemed him insane and attempted to keep him committed in an asylum, only to have him manage an escape from confinement.

Garfield went on to narrowly edge Winfield Scott Hancock in the election, and Guiteau, harboring delusions of grandeur, believed he had helped tip the scales in Garfield's favor. As such, he believed that he was entitled to a post in Garfield's nascent administration, perhaps even an ambassadorship, and he continued to rack up debts while operating under the assumption that he would soon have the government salary to pay them back. However, despite lobbying around Republican headquarters in New York City and even approaching Cabinet members, no post was forthcoming for the troubled man. Eventually, in May 1881, Secretary of State James Blaine told him to never show up again. Enraged by the perceived slight, Guiteau bought a revolver and plotted to kill the president. He got his chance on July 2, 1881 at a railroad station, shooting Garfield in the back twice and bragging to the authorities, "I am a Stalwart of the Stalwarts...Arthur is president now!"

Garfield would live for nearly three more months, and the poor standards of medical care in the 1880s would end up being responsible for the fact he did not survive wounds that he would've survived at the end of the 19th century. Indeed, Guiteau would cite medical malpractice at trial, stating, "I deny the killing, if your honor please. We admit the shooting." Those kinds of statements and his generally odd behavior helped ensure Guiteau's lawyers would claim he was insane, one of the first high profile attempts to use that as a defense against a crime. However, that never had much chance of succeeding, and claims of insanity were heartily rejected by prosecutors.

Garfield was the second president to be assassinated after Abraham Lincoln, and today he is often remembered as one of the presidents to die in office after being elected every 20 years starting with William Henry Harrison's 1840 election through John F. Kennedy's 1960 election. *James Garfield: The Life and Legacy of the Second President to Be Assassinated* chronicles the life and death of the president. Along with pictures and a bibliography, you will learn about Garfield like never before.

**Garfield's Early Years**

"It has occurred to me that the thing you have, that all men have enough of, is perhaps the thing that you care for the best, and that is your leisure - the leisure you have to think; the leisure you have to be let alone; the leisure you have to throw the plummet into your mind, and sound the depth and dive for things below." - Garfield

James Abram Garfield was born on November 19, 1831 in a log cabin in Orange Township, Ohio, the youngest child of Abram Garfield and Eliza Ballou Garfield. Garfield could trace his ancestry back to one Edward Garfield, who emigrated to the Massachusetts Bay Colony from Chester, England in 1636. Edward settled in Watertown, Massachusetts, and in the words of an early Garfield biographer, Benson Lossing, "Edward Garfield was one of the one hundred and six proprietors of Watertown, and in the ancient little cemetery there the remains of five of the late President's family name were buried. These names may yet be deciphered on the moss-grown and mouldering headstones of their graves. These seem to have been all tillers of the soil, and bore their part in the heroic labors and sufferings of those pioneers of American civilization. Their history appears to be summed up, as far as records go, in the brief inscriptions on the tombstones. Edward Garfield, the ancestor of all, lived until he was ninety- seven years of age, which is presumptive evidence that he was of a strong physical frame, and led a life of temperance and placidity."

There is little record of the immediate descendants of Edward Garfield. Solomon Garfield, the great-grandfather of James Garfield, eventually settled in western Massachusetts. After the end of the Revolutionary War, Solomon moved with his growing family to Worcester, New York, in western New York and bought a small farm. Sometime in the 1790s, Solomon's son Thomas married Asenath Hill, who bore a son in December 1799 they named Abram, James Garfield's father. After the death of his father in 1801, Asenath turned young Abram to the care of a neighbor, James Stone, who cared for the child and for whom he later became an apprentice.

Garfield's mother, Eliza Ballou, was born in Richmond, New Hampshire, on September 21, 1801. Descended from French Huguenots, Lossing described Eliza as "like nearly all of the Ballou race, is of small stature…The Ballous have been called a 'French pony breed,' that is, of compact and tough moral, mental and physical fibre; possessed of great nervous energy, combined with untiring power of endurance. They have been marked by great conscientiousness and honesty of purpose, tenacity of will, and a thorough independence of spirit."

Around 1809, the Ballou family departed Richmond and settled in Worcester near the Garfield family. Lossing noted, "Then began the mysterious workings of God's providence; then was made the strange but unuttered prophecy of the future, fulfilled in our day. Abraham Garfield and Eliza Ballou were playfellows for several years of their childhood. As they advanced into their 'teens' their intimacy assumed a more interesting aspect. The boy of fourteen or fifteen had become gallant and chivalric toward the little maiden. He was growing up like a tall pine of the forest; she was like a sweet but vigorous flowering shrub, giving beauty and fragrance to the world in which she moved. A tender passion was budding."

Unfortunately for young love, the Ballou family moved from Worcester in 1814 and settled in Zanesville, Ohio, but at the end of his apprenticeship, Abram left for Ohio, reunited with Eliza, and married her a year later. Eventually, he moved his family to Cuyahoga county. Lossing explained, There, on a plot of fifty acres of land which he bought, he built a log cabin with one room and three windows, for a shelter and home for his wife and babies, until he should make a better one. Their nearest neighbor was seven miles distant."

It was there that the future President Garfield was born. Lossing described this early childhood home: "Abraham Garfield's home in the Orange wilderness 'was a very humble one, but it was ennobled and adorned with love and hope and high resolves. The cabin was only about twenty feet one way and thirty feet the other. The logs were as rough as when the tree fell, neither moss nor bark having been stripped off. Its door was made of rude split plank, and was hung on heavy iron strap-hinges. There were three small windows, and a board floor made smooth with a broad-axe. In the absence of nails or spikes, this floor was kept in its place by timbers laid across each end. The logs of the house were rudely dove-tailed together by an axe wielded by Garfield's skillful hands. The chinks between the logs were filled with wet clay, and so, also, was the wooden chimney that arose at the end of it made tight. It was made comfortable in winter and summer; and it scarcely had a rival in beauty, spaciousness and convenience in all that region."

**A replica of the log cabin**

In late 1833, a fire broke out in the woods surrounding their farm. In an effort to save his home and his fields, Abram fought the fire himself, spending the entire day at the effort. In the end, Abram saved his farm, but it came at a heavy cost. According to Lossing, "On entering his cabin at sunset, Garfield's physical powers were well-nigh exhausted by fatigue, and, dreadfully over-heated, he soon felt his whole frame trembling with a mortal chill. His alarmed wife covered him with blankets, but without seeming effect at first. For nearly forty hours he suffered greatly, when either a casual passer-by or a quack doctor recommended him to have a blister placed on his inflamed throat. Almost instantly the trouble there was increased, and in the course of a few hours he died of suffocation — possibly of congestion of the lungs. He was then only thirty-three years of age and in full possession of his great bodily strength. It is related that just before he died he arose, walked to the door, spoke to his cattle, and as he returned and seated himself on his bed, just able to speak, he commended his little ones to the tender care of their mother, and expired. His body was laid in a corner of the wheat-field."

Eliza was left alone in what was still wilderness, far from neighbors and nowhere near family, with four children, including two-year-old James. By all accounts a strong-willed woman, she succeeded in keeping her family together and managed to eke out a poor living on their farm. She sold 50 of their 80 acres to settle her husband's debts and pay off the mortgage on the farm.

As the surrounding neighborhood became more populated, Eliza offered a part of her property for a schoolhouse, which was promptly built and staffed with a schoolmaster. Eager for all of her children to receive an education, Eliza sent all of them, including James when he was four-years-old.

Lossing described what James was like as a child: "James was a restless boy from the beginning. Perpetual motion when awake characterized him. One of the rigid rules of his first school-master, the New Hampshire youth, was that boys and girls must sit still in school. James tried to do it, for he wished to be dutiful, but in his eagerness and effort to be obedient he neglected his studies. His teacher complained to his mother that he would not sit still and did not learn. The mother was grieved, and her evident disappointment troubled the little fellow, who promised to try to do better. He tried hard, but in vain. Motion and learning, quiet and a block of wood, appeared to be synonymous terms. The Yankee wit of the teacher soon solved the difficulty. He allowed James to move about as much as he pleased, when the -boy shot ahead in acquirements which won for him the prize of the New Testament for his excellence in reading, as above mentioned. In a very few days after this change of treatment the teacher was enabled to say to his mother, 'James is perpetual motion, but he learns; and not a scholar in the school learns so fast as he.' When James carried home the New Testament as a reward for his diligence and progress, Widow Garfield's cottage was full of delight."

As James grew, so did his thirst for knowledge. By the time he was 12, he was not only working as a carpenter but continued his studies at home under his mother's careful tutelage. Indeed, Eliza was the greatest influence on his life, particularly his life of faith. Lossing explained, "Better than all this book knowledge, James Garfield, under the judicious teachings of his mother, became thoroughly imbued with strong religious feelings, and had the germ of a pure faith implanted in his heart so soon as his intellect began to bud and blossom. How general is the rale that 'Great men are the sons of great mothers.' In this category may be ranked as a bright illustration of the rule, Eliza Garfield and her illustrious son. Religion, 'pure and undefiled before God and man,' was a part of that mother's nature. It was her family inheritance."

Eliza and her late husband had become members of the Church of Christ, one of the sects of "Campbellites" founded on the frontier in by the preacher Alexander Campbell in the late 1820s. According to Lossing, Campbell's main emphasis was on the Bible as the sole basis for Christian faith: "Mrs. Garfield was a diligent student of the Holy Scriptures. A Disciples' meeting-house had been established about three miles from her home, to which she and her children walked every Sabbath, when not too stormy, for years, to engage in public worship. She caused her children also to be great Bible readers, and with the aid of its teachings she educated her household in the purest principles of morality, which made every word or deed darkened with the lightest shade of indecency hateful to her and them in a degree not to be described. Yet she was by no means an austere woman or a prude. There was never seen any of the forbidding aspects of asceticism in her home. On the contrary, she was a woman of uncommon cheerfulness of temper;

fond of innocent merriment; an excellent singer of a great variety of hymns, songs and ballads, and filled her home with music from morning until night."

**Campbell**

At 16, James struck out on his own. Moving to Cleveland, he tried to get a job on one of the vessels plying Lake Erie, but ultimately, the only position he could get was on a canal boat captained by his cousin, Amos Letcher. Letcher employed James for the *Evening Star*, where he was put in charge of the mules pulling the boat through the Erie Canal. Letcher would later recount a story of Garfield during this period to Edmund Kirke, who wrote a brief campaign biography of Garfield: "At Eleven Mile Lock we changed teams. Another hand took the tow-path, and Jim, with his team, came on board. After he had taken care of his team Jim came up on deck, and I thought I would sound him a little on the rudiments of geography, arithmetic, and grammar, for I was just green enough in those days to imagine that I knew it all. You see, I had been a teacher for three winters in the backwoods of Steuben county, Indiana. 'Jim, 'I said, 'I hear there is some come-out to you, and if you have no objections I would like to make up my own mind in regard to it. As it is a long way to Pancake Lock, this will be a good time; so I should like to ask you a few questions.' 'Proceed,' said Jim, 'but don't ask too hard ones.' I asked him several and he answered them all, and then turned on me, and asked me several that I could not answer, and I was like the boy who got into a row and said, 'If you'll let me alone, I'll let you alone.' Jim,' I said, 'you have too good a head on you to be a wood-chopper or a canal -driver. You go to school one term more, and you will be qualified to teach a common school, and then you can make anything you have a mind to out of yourself.' 'Do you think so, captain?' And it set him a thinking, I know. 'Everything went off well until about ten o'clock that night. Then we were approaching the twenty-one locks of Akron, and I sent my bow man to make the first lock ready. Just as he got there, a bow man from a boat above appeared and said, 'Don't turn this lock; our boat is just around the bend, ready to enter. 'But my man objected and commenced turning the gate. By this time both boats were near the lock, with their head-lights shining as bright as day, and every man from both was on hand, ready for a field fight. I motioned to my bow man, and asked, 'Were you here first?' 'It is hard to tell,' he replied, 'but we will have the lock anyhow.' 'All right; just as you say,' I said; and we laid out for a battle. 'Jim had heard what had been said, and, tapping me on the shoulder, he said, 'See here, captain, does that lock belong to us P 'I really suppose, according to law, it does not; but we will have it anyhow.' 'No,' replied the boy, 'we will not.' 'And why not?' I asked, in surprise. 'Because it does not belong to us.' I saw that Jim was right, so I cried, 'Boys, let them have the lock.' At sunrise next morning we had got through all the twenty-one locks, and were on Summit Lake. It was a fine morning. The other driver was cracking his whip over his leader, had got them to a trot, and all seemed to be in good humor. Breakfast was called. George Lee, our steersman, came out and sat down to breakfast, and the first word he spoke was, 'Jim, what is the matter with you?' 'Nothing,' said Jim. 'I never felt better in my life.' 'But why did you go for giving up the lock last night?' 'Oh, I thought it wasn't ours.' 'Jim, you are a coward,' he answered; 'you ain't fit for a boatman. You may do to chop wood or milk cows, but a man or a boy isn't fit for a boat who won't fight for his rights. 'Jim didn't make any answer.'"

**Garfield at 16**

After six weeks, Garfield came down with an illness that was thought to be malaria, so he was taken home, where his mother nursed him back to health for the next several months. During this time, she persuaded Garfield to not return to the canal and instead head back to school, in part because she hoped he would become a teacher at least part of the year. In this she was assisted by a young schoolmaster in their neighborhood. Thus, when he was fully recovered, in the spring of 1849, Garfield entered Geauga Seminary in Chester, Ohio.

In 1867, Garfield wrote a letter to the trustees of the Seminary recalling his experiences there: "In the winter of 1848-9 I was at my mother's house in Orange, Cuyahoga county, Ohio, suffering from a three months' siege of fever and ague, which I had brought from the Ohio canal the preceding summer. Samuel D. Bates, now a distinguished minister of the gospel in Marion, Ohio, was that winter teaching the district school near my mother's. He had attended the seminary at Chester, and urged several of the young men in the neighborhood to return there with him in the spring. Being yet too ill to return to my plan of becoming a sailor on the lake, I resolved to attend school one term and post pone sailing until autumn. Accordingly, I joined two other young men, and, with the necessary provisions for boarding ourselves, we reached Chester, March 6, 1849, and rented a room in an unpainted frame house nearly west from the seminary and across the street from it. I bought the second algebra I ever saw, and commenced the study of it there. Studied also natural philosophy and grammar. I attended there in the fall of 1849, and during the following winter taught my first school. Returned to the seminary again in the spring of 1850. I commenced the study of Latin and finished algebra and botany. At the close of the spring term I made my first public speech. It was a six minutes' oration at the annual exhibition. My diary shows the anxiety and solicitude through which I passed in its preparation and delivery. During the summer vacation of 1850 1 worked at the carpenter's trade in Chester. Among other things, I helped to build a two-story house on the east side of the road, a little way south of the seminary grounds. Attended school during the fall term of 1850, and commenced the study of Greek. Worked mornings, evenings and Saturdays at my trade, and thus paid my way. After the first term at Chester I never received any pecuniary assistance. The cost of living, however, was much less than it now is. In my second term at Chester I had board, lodging and washing for one dollar and six cents per week."

A description of Garfield during this time came from an acquaintance who met him once at the home of a mutual friend: "He was rather shabbily but neatly clad. He appeared like a fast-growing lad, for he was then five feet ten inches in height. He was dressed in pantaloons much too short for him, reaching only half-way down the legs of his well-worn cowskin boots. They were made of coarse grey satinet. His waistcoat of serge cloth was much too short for him; and his coat, of similar material, was worn threadbare, and the sleeves reached only to a point half-way between the elbows and the wrists. Ilis head (which bore an abundance of yellow hair— real 'Saxon locks') was covered by a drab slouched hat without a band; and his shirt, as it appeared at the neck and sleeves, was spotless white linen, made from flax raised on his mother's little farm, and spun with her own hands. His eyes were blue, his complexion ruddy, his forehead was expansive, and there was strength and intelligence in every feature. He was there on an errand for his mother. He stood with his hat off, and his whole head and facial expression struck me as most remarkable. When he departed I said to my friend, 'That boy will make a noise in the world.'"

While at Geauga, two events occurred to shape Garfield's future. Unusual for educational institutions in the 19th century, Geauga was a co-educational institution. While there, he met Lucretia Rudolph, described by Lossing as "a modest, retiring, bright and studious girl." It began as a casual acquaintance, but their meeting would be the foundation for a much deeper relationship that would later result in their marriage.

Furthermore, around this time, Garfield underwent a profound religious conversion. He had dutifully attended religious services with his mother, more out of a desire to please than to worship God, but in March 1850 he attended a camp meeting. Lossing described its effects: "At length a wise old man, possessed of great good sense and straightforward simplicity of character and speech, held meetings in the school-house. His ministrations first aroused the fixed attention of the young school master, and then touched his heart. The young man sought an interview with the preacher. 'If I could be satisfied,' he said, 'that what you have taught to-night is simple truth and would secure happiness, I would embrace the faith." The next evening the preacher spoke in a special manner to such doubters. Garfield was convinced, and then and there he publicly acknowledged his convictions. He soon became a full member of the church his mother so much loved and adorned. He was baptized in a small tributary of the Chagrin River. A new light illumined his mind and invigorated his heart. 'My best life,' said young Garfield, 'shall henceforth be given to the task of accomplishing the salvation of my fellow-mortals from degradation and unhappiness. I will master learning and so fit myself for the work.'"

After he left Geauga in 1851 in order to prepare himself to enter college, Garfield enrolled at the Western Reserve Eclectic Institute in Hiram, Oho, a school run by the Disciples of Christ (another Campbellite sect), which he attended until 1854. Garfield later wrote, "I had never seen a geometry, and, regarding both teacher and class with a feeling of reverential awe for the intellectual height to which they had climbed, I studied their faces so closely that I seem to see them now as distinctly as I saw them then. And it has been my good fortune since that time to claim them all as intimate friends. The teacher was Thomas Munnell, and the members of his class were William B. Hazen, George A. Baker and Almeda A. Booth."

In order to pay for his studies, which included Greek and Latin, he took a position as a janitor. But because of his obvious talents he was hired to teach while still a student. In addition, he preached at several churches when the ministers were absent. An early biographical sketch portrays the hard-working young Garfield during these years: "He began at Hiram in the fall of 1851, with but twenty-four weeks of Latin and twelve weeks of Greek. He taught for two winters in the district school. After the first term he taught constantly from three to six, and later, the whole six classes, so that he could only study nights and mornings. In June, 1854 — less than three years after he went to Hiram — he not only had fitted himself to enter college, but had completed two years of the college course, so as to be admitted in the junior class in Williams, in full and good standing. He not only paid his way as he went, and supported himself, but had ' saved up ' about $350. If there is any precedent for such achievements I never saw or heard of it. " It is impossible to overestimate the forming character of the studies thus athletically pursued, at such a period of Garfield's life, with such singular enthusiasm and in such inspiring and elevating and refining companionship. Such a combination of circumstances, influences and associations was far more valuable to the formation of the tastes, tendencies, aspirations, sentiments and principles of the future soldier and statesman than the most famous universities of the world could have supplied. Mind and heart were simultaneously quickened and demitting to the influence and instruction of a noble woman." It was during this time that Lucretia Rudolph entered Geauga as a student, and Garfield happened to tutor her in Greek.

**Lucretia in the 1870s**

After his graduation from Geauga, Garfield opted to attend Williams College in Massachusetts instead of the Disciples of Christ College in Virginia established by Alexander Campbell. He later explained his decision in a letter, which reveals his opposition to slavery : "There are three reasons why I have decided not to go to Bethany: 1st. The course of study is not so extensive or thorough as in Eastern colleges. 2d. Bethany leans too heavily toward slavery. 3d. I am the son of Disciple parents, am one myself, and have had but little acquaintance with people of other views; and having always lived in the West, I think it will make me more liberal, both in my religious and general views and sentiments, to go into a new circle, where I shall be under new influences. These considerations led me to conclude to go to some New England college. I therefore wrote to the Presidents of Brown University, Yale, and Williams,' setting forth the amount of study I had done, and asking how long it would take me to finish their course." Before departing for Williams in 1854, Garfield and Lucretia Rudolph were betrothed.

"The lesson of history is rarely learned by the actors themselves." - Garfield

Because of the extensive work he had already done, Garfield enrolled at Williams as a third-year student, and it was there that he gave his first political speech, one in support of John C. Fremont for President of the United States in 1856. By 1853 and 1854, Henry Clay's Compromise of 1850 came under withering assault, because the Compromise had not settled all territory needed to be admitted for statehood. In an attempt to organize the center of North America – Kansas and Nebraska – without offsetting the slave-free balance, Senator Stephen Douglas of Illinois proposed the Kansas-Nebraska Act.

Kansas-Nebraska proved to be the straw that broke the camel's back. First, the Kansas-Nebraska Act eliminated the Missouri Compromise line of 1820, which the Compromise of 1850 had maintained and had stipulated for over a generation that states north of the line would be free and states south of it *could* have slavery. This was essential to maintaining the balance of slave and free states in the Union. The Kansas-Nebraska Act, however, ignored the line completely and proposed that all new territories be organized by popular sovereignty. Settlers could vote whether they wanted their state to be slave or free.

When popular sovereignty became the standard in Kansas and Nebraska, the primary result was that thousands of zealous pro-slavery and anti-slavery advocates both moved to Kansas to influence the vote, creating a dangerous and ultimately deadly mix. Numerous attacks took place between the two sides, and many pro-slavery Missourians organized attacks on Kansas towns just across the border.

While men like John Brown acted militantly in the territories, politicians across the North, primarily Whigs and Free Soilers, were aghast over the Kansas-Nebraska Act. The suggestion that Congress could extend slavery into any unsettled territory violated some of their dearest held principles that slavery should not extend further. Whigs and Free Soilers in the North quickly coalesced against the "Slave Power", believing Southern influence in Washington had gone too far and now held the government in a strangle-hold. This coalescence first became known as the "anti-Nebraska" group, but it quickly vowed to form a new political party dedicated to keeping the Western territories free from slavery.

Ultimately, Fremont, best known as "The Pathfinder" for his historic expeditions to the West, was nominated as the first Republican candidate for the presidency, slated to run in the 1856 election. His strong abolitionist views appealed to many in the newly formed party, his name recognition was certainly a strong positive, and his experience in California politics gave him significant (albeit brief) political experience. One of the campaign slogans encapsulated it all: "Free Soil, Free Men, and Fremont." Ultimately, however, Fremont lost to James Buchanan.

Meanwhile, Garfield completed his course work in two years, graduating Phi Beta Kappa in August 1856 as Salutatorian. Returning to Ohio after graduation, he was hired as Professor of Ancient Languages at Hiram College in Hiram, Ohio. In addition to teaching, he occasionally preached in the churches of the Disciples of Christ around Hiram and delivered political speeches. In addition, he read for the law, gaining admittance to the bar of Cuyahoga County in 1860. In 1857, Garfield was appointed president of the college itself.

After becoming the college's president, Garfield married Lucretia Rudolph. Lossing went into more detail about their courtship and her background: "Lucretia was the daughter of an eastern farmer of German descent, named Zebulon Rudolph, who had settled in Cuyahoga county, Ohio. Her mother was Arabella Mason, a descendant of an old Connecticut family, but a native of Hartford, Windsor county, Vermont. They were thrifty people, appreciated the advantages of education, and gave Lucretia every opportunity in their power to acquire knowledge, which the region afforded. She and young Garfield were married on November 11, 1858, by the Rev. Dr. Hitchcock, President of the Western Reserve College at Hudson, Ohio. A neat little cottage was bought by him in front of the college at Hiram, and there their most happy wedded life was begun in a very humble way. They had very few of this world's goods, but were very rich in love, mutual tastes, energy, love of knowledge and perfect accord in sentiment upon all questions of life."

The growing controversy over slavery spurred Garfield's further forays into politics, and he subsequently became a speaker for Republicans and other anti-slavery candidates throughout the area. In 1859, the local Republican party nominated him as their candidate for the state senate, and he was elected by a large majority. He served in that office until the outbreak of the Civil War in 1861, and in that role, he was appointed to extend an invitation to the governors of Tennessee and Kentucky to visit Ohio. Traveling to Louisville, where the two men were gathered to celebrate the completion of the Louisville and Nashville Railroad in 1860, he delivered a speech which read in part, "Brethren, we have too long heard of the North and the South. Their angry words have too long vexed the hearts of our fellow-citizens. But there is a third voice to be heard ere long. I hope and believe the day is not far distant when the great West shall speak, and. that voice shall be heard from sea to sea. In that voice shall be heard no terms of doubt or uncertainty; no note of disunion shall be heard in that utterance."

As 1860 went on, Garfield observed with increasing dismay the rhetoric from Southern politicians arguing for secession in order to preserve what they considered their rights to slavery. He expressed his views in a Fourth of July speech he gave at Ravenna, Ohio that year: "We have seen that our Republic differs in its origin from all the monarchies of the world. We may also see that it differs widely from all other republics of ancient or modern times. These all centered round a conquering hero or a powerful city — ours round a principle. In the brightest days of the Grecian Republic, its strength and glory rested upon the life and fortunes of Pericles. In the old Dutch Republic of Holland and the later establishments of modern Germany, freedom was of the city and not of the people. The burghers were the only free men, and they constituted an aristocracy more haughty and imperious than the hereditary peers of England. The peasants of the rural districts, the toiling thousands, were hardly known to the government, except that they bore many of its heavy burdens. But here, cities are not tyrannies, and freedom in her best estate is found in the green fields of the country, among the hardy tillers of the soil. Heroes did not make our liberties, they but reflected and illustrated them. Individuals may wear for a time the glory of our institutions, but they carry it not with them to the grave. Like rain-drops from heaven, they pass through the circle of the shining bow and add to its lustre, but when they have sunk in the earth again, the proud arch still spans the sky and shines gloriously on, Governments, in general, look upon man only as a citizen, a fraction of the state. God looks upon him as an individual man, with capacities, duties and a destiny of his own; and just in proportion as a government recognizes the individual and shields him in the exercises of his rights, in that proportion is it Godlike and glorious. The village church and the village school have become our great civilizing and elevating guardians, and we men tion with honest pride the fact that more than half of all the revenue of our State Government is annually expended in the education of our youth. And yet there are other States in the Union which, in this respect, wear still brighter laurels than Ohio. To all these means of culture is added that powerful incentive to personal ambition which springs from the genius of our Government. The pathway to honorable distinction lies open to all. No post of honor so high but the poorest boy may hope to reach it."

Ironically, the first Republican President was one of the most fervent Whig holdouts in the mid-1850s. Although destined to be forever associated with the Republican Party, Abraham Lincoln wasn't yet convinced that the Party of Clay was on its last legs when the Republican Party first began to form. The one term Congressman ran as a Whig for Senate in 1854, and it was only after that loss that Lincoln began to gather among Republican circles.

Going into the Republican Convention in May 1860, the Republicans were hopeful. The Democratic Party, partly because of Stephen Douglas, was deeply divided over slavery, and it had broken into a Northern and Southern faction. By dividing their votes, they were likely handing over the presidency to a Republican Party that would barely win a plurality across the nation. Sensing opportunity, the Republicans were careful in selecting their candidate. Many delegates considered the frontrunner, William H. Seward, to be too radical. With a divided electorate, there were fears that Seward's radicalism might lose the Midwest for the Republicans.

At the Convention, Seward's support maintained steady throughout the rounds of voting, but Abraham Lincoln polled a surprising second place on the first ballot. He gradually picked up votes from other Midwestern candidates until he was selected as the Republican Party's Presidential nominee on the third ballot. Hannibal Hamlin of Maine was nominated as the Vice Presidential nominee.

Lincoln had essentially been chosen for his moderate stance on slavery. Unlike many other viable Republican contenders, Lincoln was less likely to alienate valuable "battleground" states like Illinois, Indiana and Ohio. At the same time, the more staunchly abolitionist Northeast would have no better alternative.

Throughout the fall, the campaign broiled on. As was customary, Lincoln did no active campaigning. Presidential candidates in the mid-19th century did not campaign on their own behalf; surrogates did the work for them. His supporters portrayed Lincoln as a man of great integrity from humble origins. Opponents conjured up the image of a radical Black Republican. Evidently, such language sold well in the South. By mid-summer, talk of Southern secession if Lincoln were elected was commonplace. Lincoln himself took none of this chatter seriously: he thought it to be nothing more than the usual political sensationalism.

**Lincoln in 1860**

Nevertheless, the election of 1860 was held under extraordinary circumstances, and the results were equally unprecedented. Four candidates competed, and each of the candidates won some electoral votes. While the Republicans nominated Abraham Lincoln, the Democrats nominated Stephen Douglas, the Southern Democrats chose John C. Breckinridge and the Constitutional Union Party selected John Bell of Tennessee as its nominee. The Constitutional Union Party was compromised of former Know-Nothings and Whigs in the middle states of Kentucky, Tennessee and Virginia who advocated compromise and unity on the issue of slavery.

The race was so fractured that Lincoln only appeared on the ballot in five slave states: Virginia, Kentucky, Maryland, Delaware and Missouri. In Virginia, Lincoln only won about 1% of the vote, and in all the other slave states where Lincoln was on the ballot he finished no better than third. Lincoln won only two counties out all 996 counties in the 15 slave states, but Lincoln and the Republicans won decisively in the Electoral College, with 180 of the 303 votes cast and 152 needed for a majority. In the popular vote, however, Lincoln only garnered 39%, but came out nearly half a million votes ahead of his next nearest competitor, the Little Giant, Stephen Douglas. In the Electoral College, Douglas only won 12 votes with a single state – Missouri. Lincoln swept the North, Breckinridge took the South, and Bell won most of the middle. The results reflected the great regional divide, and the nation was set for Civil War.

After the election, South Carolina announced its secession from the Union in December 1860, and it was soon followed by other states in the Deep South. Garfield, still in the state legislature, led the efforts to prepare Ohio for what he saw as the inevitable conflict between the Union and the new Confederate States of America. He spoke in support of a Militia Bill to raise and equip 6,000 men on January 24, 1861: "If by coercion it is meant that the Federal Government shall declare and wage war against a State, then I have yet to see any man, Democrat or Republican, who is a coercionist. But, if by the term it is meant that the Genera] Government shall enforce the laws, by whomsoever violated, shall protect the property and flag of the Union, shall punish traitors to the Constitution, be they ten men or ten thousand, then I am a coercionist. Every member of the Senate, by his vote on the eighth resolution, is a coercionist. Nine-tenths of the people of Ohio are coercionists. Every man is a coercionist or a traitor."

In a letter to President Hinsdale at Williams College, written about the same time, he wrote, "My heart and thoughts are full almost every moment with the terrible reality of our country's condition. We have learned so long to look upon the convulsions of European States as things wholly impossible here, that the people are slow in coming to the belief that there may be any breaking up of our institutions; but stern, awful certainty is fastening upon the hearts of men. I do not see any way, outside a miracle of God, which can avoid civil war with all its attendant horrors. Peaceable dissolution is utterly impossible. Indeed, I cannot say that I would wish it possible. To make the concessions demanded by the South would be hypocritical and sinful; they would neither be obeyed nor respected. I am inclined to believe that the sin of slavery is one of which it may be said that without the shedding of blood there is no remission. " All that is left us as a State, or say, as a company of Northern States, is to arm and prepare to defend ourselves and the Federal Government. I believe the doom of slavery is drawing near. Let war come, and the slaves will get the vague notion that it is waged for them, and a magazine will be lighted whose explosion will shake the whole fabric of slavery. Even if all this happen, I cannot yet abandon the belief that one government will rule this continent, and its people be one people."

In February, Lincoln passed through Columbus on the way to his inauguration in Washington. Garfield, writing to Hinsdale on February 16, gave his impressions of the new president: "Mr. Lincoln has come and gone. The rush of people to see him at every point on the route is astonishing. The reception here was plain and republican, but very impressive. He has been raising a respectable pair of dark brown whiskers, which decidedly improve his looks, but no appendage can ever render him remarkable for beauty. On the whole I am greatly pleased with him. He clearly shows his want of culture, and the marks of Western life, but there is no touch of affectation in him, and he has a peculiar power of impressing yon that he is frank, direct and thoroughly honest. His remarkable good sense, simple and condensed style of expression, and evident marks of indomitable will, give me great hopes for the country. And, after the long, dreary period of Buchanan's weakness and cowardly imbecility, the people will hail a strong and vigorous leader."

Lincoln made his way to Washington and was duly inaugurated on March 4, 1861. A little over a month later, on April 12, 1861, Confederate forces bombarded Fort Sumter in Charleston Harbor, forcing its surrender the next day, and in response, Lincoln issued a call to the states to supply militia to suppress the rebellion. Garfield supported a bill in the Ohio Legislature to appropriate $1 million in response to Governor William Dennison, Jr.'s message announcing Lincoln's call for troops. The message concluded, "But as the contest may grow to greater dimensions than is now anticipated, 1 deem it my duty to recommend to the General Assembly of this State to make provisions proportionate to its means to assist the National authorities in restoring the integrity and strength of the Union, in all its amplitude, as the only means of preserving the rights of all the States, and insuring the permanent peace and prosperity of the whole country. I earnestly recommend, also, than an appropriation of not less than four hundred and fifty thousand dollars he immediately made for the purchase of arms and equipments for the use of the volunteer militia of the State. I need not remind you of the pressing exigency for the prompt organization and arming of the military force of the State."

**Dennison**

To lead the forces, members of the Ohio Legislature resigned their positions, including the acting Speaker, and accepted appointment as officers. In this regard, Garfield was no different - he set to work raising a company of volunteers from among the students at Hiram College, which proved to be the nucleus of the 42nd Regiment of the Ohio Volunteers. Governor Dennison appointed Garfield the Lieutenant-Colonel of this regiment, and after five weeks of training Garfield presented his unit as ready for service. He was commissioned as a Colonel on August 14, 1861.

The regiment was formally organized at Camp Chase near Columbus, a process completed on November 26. On December 14, the regiment received orders to report for service in the Department of the Ohio at Prestonsburg. Kentucky. Garfield sent the troops forward and traveled to Louisville to report to General Don Carols Buell at his headquarters. F. H. Mason, in his history of the Ohio 42nd Regiment, described the meeting: "On the evening of the 16th, Colonel Garfield reached Louisville and sought General Buell at his headquarters. He found a cold, silent, austere man, who asked a few direct questions, revealed nothing, and eyed the newcomer with a curious, searching expression, as though trying to look into the untried Colonel, and divine whether he would succeed or fail. Taking a map, General Buell pointed out- the position of Marshall's forces in Eastern Kentucky, marked the location in which the Union troops in that district were posted, explained the nature of .the country and its supplies, and then dismissed his visitor with the remark: ' If you were in command of the sub- department of Eastern Kentucky, what would you do? Come here to-morrow morning at nine o'clock and tell me.' "Colonel Garfield returned to his hotel, procured a map of Kentucky, the last census report, paper, pen and ink, and sat down to his task. He studied the roads, re sources, and population of every comity in Eastern Kentucky. At daylight he was still at work, but at nine o'clock he was at General Buoll's headquarters with a sketch of his plans. Buell read it and made it the basis of his Special Order ~No. 35, Army of the Ohio, December 17, 1861, by which the Eighteenth Brigade, Army of the Ohio, was organized."

**Buell**

   Appointing Garfield to the command of the 18th Brigade, which included the 42$^{nd}$ and 40th Ohio Infantry, two regiments of Kentucky infantry, and 300 men of the Second Virginia Cavalry, Buell ordered Garfield to drive the Confederate forces under Brigadier General Humphrey Marshall out of eastern Kentucky.

**Garfield during the war**

Departing Catlettsburg, Kentucky in mid-December, they marched through the valley of the Big Sandy River. Reaching Paintsville on January 7, 1862, Garfield took possession of the town the following morning. That evening, Garfield led the 42nd Ohio and two companies of the 14th Kentucky against a fortified position held by Marshall three miles south of Paintsville, but when his force arrived, Garfield discovered the post abandoned.

On January 9, 1862, Garfield led his troops in the only pitched battle he personally commanded during the war, the Battle of Middle Creek. Lossing described the action: "At about noon on the 9th, Colonel Garfield, with eleven hundred infantry from the Forty-Second Ohio and other regiments, and about six hundred cavalry, started in pursuit of Marshall, and about nine o'clock in the evening the advance was fired upon by Marshall's pickets, on the summit of Abbott's Hill. Garfield took possession of the hill, bivouacked for the night, and the next morning continued the pursuit, overtaking the enemy at the forks of Middle Creek, three miles southwest of Prestonsburg. Marshall's force consisted of about three thousand five hundred men, infantry and cavalry, with three pieces of artillery strongly posted on a hill. Major Pardee, with four hundred men, was sent across Middle Creek to attack Marshall directly in front, and Lieutenant-Colonel Monroe (Twenty-Second Kentucky) was directed to attack on Mar shall's right flank. The fight at once opened with considerable spirit, and Pardee and Monroe became hotly engaged with a force four times as large as their own. They held their ground with great obstinacy and bravery until reinforcements readied the field, when the enemy commenced to fall back. The National forces slept upon their arms, and at early dawn a reconnaissance disclosed the fact that Marshall had burned his stores and had again fled, leaving a portion of his dead on the field."

**A picture of the battlefield**

Though it was a small battle, especially compared with the later battles of the war involving far larger forces, Middle Creek represented one of the first major Union victories. The early months of the war had mostly brought a string of victories for the Confederacy, leaving supporters of the Union in despair over their cause. Mason noted, "The story of Garfield's success at Middle Creek came, therefore, like a benediction to the Union cause. Though won at a trifling cost, it was decisive so far as concerned the purposes of that immediate campaign. Marshall's force was driven from Kentucky, and made no further attempt to occupy the Sandy Valley. The important victories at Mill Spring, Forts Donaldson and Henry, and the repulse at Shiloh, followed. The victory at Mill Creek proved the first wave of a returning tide."

For his part, Garfield was humble in evaluating his first experience of battlefield command: "It was a very rash and imprudent affair on my part. If I had been an officer of more experience, I should not have made the attack. As it was, having gone into the army with the notion that fighting was our business, I didn't know any better."

Not suprrisingly, General Buell and the authorities in Washington had a different evaluation of Garfield's performance. On January 20, Buell issued the following General Order: "The general commanding takes occasion to thank General Garfield and his troops for their successful campaign against the rebel force under General Marshall, on the Big Sandy, and their gallant conduct in battle. They have overcome formidable difficulties in the character of country, condition of the roads, and the inclemency of the season; and, without artillery, have in several engagements, terminating in the battle of Middle Creek, on the 10th inst. , driven the enemy from his intrenched position, and forced him back into the mountains, with a loss of a large amount of baggage and stores, and many of his men killed or captured. These services have called into action the highest qualities of a soldier — fortitude, perseverance and courage."

On January 10, the War Department gave Garfield a commission as Brigadier-General of Volunteers, making him the youngest general in the Union. He was given command of the 20th Brigade of the Army of the Ohio, and in early 1862 he was ordered to join Major General Ulysses S. Grant's forces in their advance on Corinth, Mississippi.

Garfield's troops arrived in time to participate in the Battle of Shiloh, the biggest battle in American history at the time it was fought in April 1862. After Union General Ulysses S. Grant captured Fort Henry and Fort Donelson in early 1862, Confederate General Albert Sidney Johnston, widely considered the Confederacy's best general, concentrated his forces in northern Georgia and prepared for a major offensive that culminated with the biggest battle of the war to that point, the Battle of Shiloh. On the morning of April 6, Johnston directed an all out attack on Grant's army around Shiloh Church, and though Grant's men had been encamped there, they had failed to create defensive fortifications or earthworks. They were also badly caught by surprise. With nearly 45,000 Confederates attacking, Johnston's army began to steadily push Grant's men back toward the river.

As fate would have it, the Confederates may have been undone by friendly fire at Shiloh. Johnston advanced out ahead of his men on horseback while directing a charge near a peach orchard when he was hit in the lower leg by a bullet that historians now widely believe was fired by his own men. Nobody thought the wound was serious, including Johnston, who continued to aggressively lead his men and even sent his personal physician to treat wounded Union soldiers taken captive. But the bullet had clipped an artery, and shortly after being wounded Johnston began to feel faint in the saddle. With blood filling up his boot, Johnston unwittingly bled to death. The delay caused by his death, and the transfer of command to subordinate P.G.T. Beauregard, bought the Union defenders critical time on April 6, and the following day Grant's reinforced army struck back and pushed the Confederate army off the field.

The Battle of Shiloh lasted two days, but the battle over the battle had just begun. Grant's army had just won the biggest battle in the history of North America, with nearly 24,000 combined casualties among the Union and Confederate forces. Usually the winner of a major battle is hailed as a hero, but Grant was hardly a winner at Shiloh. The Battle of Shiloh took place before costlier battles at places like Antietam and Gettysburg, so the extent of the casualties at Shiloh shocked the nation. Moreover, at Shiloh the casualties were viewed as needless; Grant was pilloried for allowing the Confederates to take his forces by surprise, as well as the failure to build defensive earthworks and fortifications, which nearly resulted in a rout of his army. Speculation again arose that Grant had a drinking problem, and some even assumed he was drunk during the battle. Though the Union won, it was largely viewed that their success owed to the heroics of General Sherman in rallying the men and Don Carlos Buell arriving with his army, and General Buell was happy to receive the credit at Grant's expense.

As a result of the Battle of Shiloh, Grant was demoted to second-in-command of all armies in his department, an utterly powerless position. And when word of what many considered a "colossal blunder" reached Washington, several congressmen insisted that Lincoln replace Grant in the field. Lincoln famously defended Grant, telling critics, "I can't spare this man. He fights."

That summer, Garfield became ill with jaundice and suffered significant weight loss, requiring him to return home and be nursed by his wife. Once he recovered, after several months and several offers of assignments, he became Chief of Staff for Major General William S. Rosecrans, who was then in command of the Army of the Cumberland. Thus, nearly 18 months after he had fought in what was then the biggest battle in American history at Shiloh, Garfield would be on hand for the biggest battle in the West and the second biggest battle of the entire war at Chickamauga.

In mid-September 1863, the Union Army of the Cumberland under Rosecrans had taken Chattanooga, but rather than be pushed out of the action, Army of Tennessee commander Braxton Bragg decided to stop with his 60,000 men and prepare a counterattack south of Chattanooga at a creek named Chickamauga.  To bolster his firepower, Confederate President Jefferson Davis sent 12,000 additional troops under the command of Lieutenant General James Longstreet, whose corps had just recently fought at Gettysburg in July.

On the morning of September 19, 1863, Bragg's men assaulted the Union line, which was established in a wooded area thick with underbrush along the river.  That day and the morning of the next, Bragg continue to pummel Union forces, with the battle devolving from an organized succession of coordinated assaults into what one Union soldier described as "a mad, irregular battle, very much resembling guerrilla warfare on a vast scale in which one army was bushwhacking the other, and wherein all the science and the art of war went for nothing."

Late that second morning, Rosecrans was misinformed that a gap was forming in his front line, so he responded by moving several units forward to shore it up.  What Rosecrans didn't realize, however, was that in doing so he accidentally created a quarter-mile gap in the Union center, directly in the path of Longstreet's men.  Described by one of Rosecrans' own men as "an angry flood," Longstreet's attack was successful in driving one-third of the Union Army off the field, with Rosecrans himself running all the way to Chattanooga, where he was later found weeping and seeking solace from a staff priest.

As the Confederate assault continued, George H. Thomas led the Union left wing against heavy Confederate attack even after nearly half of the Union army abandoned their defenses and retreated from the battlefield, racing toward Chattanooga.  Thomas rallied the remaining parts of the army and formed a defensive stand on Horseshoe Ridge, with more units spontaneously rallying to the new defensive line. Thomas and his men managed to hold until nightfall, when they made an orderly retreat to Chattanooga while the Confederates occupied the surrounding heights, ultimately besieging the city. Dubbed "The Rock of Chickamauga", Thomas's heroics ensured that Rosecrans' army was able to successfully retreat back to Chattanooga.

In the aftermath of the Battle of Chickamauga, several Confederate generals blamed the number of men lost during what would be the bloodiest battle of the Western Theater on Bragg's incompetence, also criticizing him for refusing to pursue the escaping Union army. General Longstreet later stated to Jefferson Davis, "Nothing but the hand of God can help as long as we have our present commander."

Of course, as poorly as Bragg fared in the aftermath, Rosecrans suffered just as much. During the ensuing Confederate siege of Chattanooga, the Union brought in Ulysses S. Grant to break the siege. As for Garfield, Chickamauga also represented the end of his military career, but not before his promotion to Major General.

**Rosecrans**

The end of Garfield's military career truly had its origins in the election of 1862. Friends had approached him in early 1862 about running for Congress from the newly-drawn 19th district. He would be able to continue his military service until late 1863, because in those days, the first Congress after an election did not meet until over a year later, so the 38th Congress he would serve in did not convene until December 1863. He was nominated at the local convention in September 1862 and went on to defeat the Democratic candidate by a two-to-one margin in October 1862.

Thus, after the Battle of Chickamauga, Garfield moved to resign his commission, doing so on December 5, 1863. General Rosencrans later recalled, "Garfield was a member of my military family during the early part of the war. When he came to my headquarters, I must confess I had a prejudice against him, as I understood he was a preacher who had gone into politics, and a man of that cast I was naturally opposed to. The more I saw of him the better I liked him, and finally I gave him his choice of a brigade, or to become my Chief of Staff. He chose the latter. His views were large, and he was possessed of a thoroughly comprehensive mind. Late in the Summer of

1863 he came to me one day, and said that he had been asked to accept the Republican nomination for Congress from the Ashtabula (O.) district, and asked my advice as to whether he ought to accept it, and whether he could do so honorably. J replied that I not only thought he could accept it with honor, but that I deemed it to be his duty to do so. 'The war is not yet over,' I said, 'nor will it be for some time to come. There will be many questions arising in Congress which require not alone statesmanlike treatment, but the advice of men having an acquaintance with military affairs will be needful; and for that and several other reasons, you would, I believe, do equally as good service to this country in Congress as in the field.'"

Soon after taking his seat in Congress, Garfield became an ally of Treasury Secretary Salmon P. Chase and identified as a member of the Radical Republicans. This section of the party was fervently opposed to slavery and believed in abolishing it altogether. Radical Republicans like Thaddeus Stevens introduced legislation to confiscate lands owned by rebels and redistribute the acreage to freed slaves. Garfield supported this legislation, but President Lincoln opposed it and threatened to veto it.

**Chase**

During the debate, Garfield delivered his maiden speech in Congress, and it advocated the measure as necessary to fully prosecute the war against the South: "Mr. Speaker, if we want a peace that is not a hollow peace we must follow that example and make thorough work of this war. We must establish freedom in the midst of servitude, and the authority of law in the midst of rebellion. We must fill the thinned ranks of our armies, assure them that a grateful and loving people are behind them, and they will go down against the enemy, bearing with them the majesty and might of a great nation. We must follow the march of the Army with a law that will sweep away the cause of the whole terrible revolution. The war began by proclamation, and it must end by proclamation. We can hold the insurgent States in military subjection half a century if need be, or until they are purged of their dross and poison, and leave them to stand up clean before the country, to come back with clean hands if they come at all. I want to see in all those States the men who have fought and suffered for the truth tilling those fields on which they pitched their tents. I want to see them, like old Kaspar of Blenheim, on the summer evenings, with their children upon their knees, and pointing out the spot where brave men fell and marble commemorates it. Let no breath of treason be whispered there. I want no man there, like one from my own State, who came before the great struggle in Georgia and gave us his views of peace. He came as the friend of Vallandigham, the man for whom the gentleman on the other side of the House from my State worked and voted. We were on the eve of the great battle. I said to him, 'You wish to make Mr. Vallandigham Governor of Ohio. Why?' 'Because, in the first place,' using the language of the gentleman from Now York [Mr. Fernando Wood,] 'you cannot subjugate the South, and we propose to withdraw without trying it any further. In the next place, we do not want anything to do with an abolition war, and will not give one dollar for that purpose.' Remember, gentlemen, what occurred on the conscription bill this morning. 'To-morrow,' I continued, 'we may be engaged in a death struggle with the rebel army that confronts us, and is daily increasing. Where is the sympathy of your party? Do you want us beaten, or Bragg beaten?' He answered they had no interest in fighting, that they did not believe in fighting."

One area where Garfield opposed the majority of his fellow Republicans concerned conscription. Financially able recruits were able to use bounties to buy their way out of military service by paying others to take their place. As someone who had left his private affairs voluntarily, Garfield saw the bounty system as inequitable. In a speech, Garfield spoke vigorously against the existing law, pointing out that of 300,000 men eligible to enlist, only 10,000 had done so, with the remaining obtaining an exemption by providing a substitute. He complained, "The bill, as my colleague on the committee has said, was presented as a whole; it is a measure that had no value in it, except the last two sections, unless taken as a whole. The heart is cut out of it, and the head cut off, and, with the exception of those two sections, I have not only no desire that it should pass, but I believe the mangled trunk would be a deformity, and would seriously injure the efficiency of the present law. Wo come before the house to say that the President had informed us, what our own examination of the state of the country also led us to believe, that the government is in want of men, and not of money, to fill the ranks of its army;

that the law we have given to the President and the War Department has in the main failed to secure the requisite reinforcements. " It is no longer a question that we cannot retain the commutation clause of the Enrollment act and at the same time fill up the army so as to supply the waste of battle. 'Gentlemen, this Congress must sooner or later meet the issue face to face, and I believe the time will soon come, if it has not now come, when we must give up the war or give up the commutation. 1 believe the men and the Congress that shall finally refuse to strike out the commutation clause, but retain it in its full force as it now is, will substantially vote to abandon the war. And I am not ready to believe, I will not believe, that the Thirty-eighth Congress has come to that conclusion.'"

A few days later, Garfield spoke in what Lossing labeled "one of the strongest speeches, it is believed, that he ever delivered in Congress." Garfield told his fellow Congressmen, "It has never been my policy to conceal a truth merely because it is unpleasant. It may be well to smile in the face of danger, but it is neither well nor wise to let danger approach unchallenged and unannounced. A brave nation, like a brave man, desires to see and measure the perils which threaten it. It is the right of the American people to know the necessities of the Republic when they are called upon to make sacrifices for it. It is this lack of confidence in ourselves and the people, this timid waiting for events to control us when they should obey us, that makes men oscillate between hope and fear; now in the sunshine of the hill-tops, and now in the gloom and shadows of the valley. To such men the bulletin which heralds success in the army gives exultation and high hope; the evening dispatch announcing some slight disaster to our advancing columns brings gloom and depression. Hope rises and falls by the accidents of war, as the mercury of the thermometer changes by the accidents of heat and cold. Let us rather take for our symbol the sailor's barometer, which faithfully forewarns him of the tempest, and gives him unerring promise of serene skies and peaceful seas."

Given Garfield's perception of Lincoln as too conciliatory towards the South, as exemplified by Lincoln's pocket veto of the Wade-Davis Bill concerning the upcoming Reconstruction, he was lukewarm concerning Lincoln's reelection. He said at one point, "He will probably be the man, though I think we could do better." In the 1864 election, Garfield was also reelected to the House, and Lincoln led the Republicans to victory.

The morning after Lincoln's assassination, on April 15, Garfield was in New York. Around 11:00 a.m., a meeting on Wall Street threatened to devolve into a riot. Into the midst strode Garfield, who told the crowd, "Fellow-citizens: Clouds and darkness are round about Him! His pavilion is dark waters and thick clouds of the skies! Justice and judgment are the establishment of His throne! Mercy and truth shall go before His face! Fellow citizens! God reigns, and the Government at Washington still lives!"

A witness to the event later reported, "The effect was tremendous. The crowd stood riveted to the ground in awe, gazing at the motionless orator, and thinking of God and of His Providence over the Government and the Nation. As the boiling wave subsides and settles to the sea when some strong wind beat it down, so the tumult of the people sank and became still. As the rod draws the electricity from the air and conducts it safely to the ground, so this man had drawn fury from that frantic crowd and guided it to more tranquil thoughts than vengeance. It was a triumph of eloquence, a flash of inspiration such as seldom comes to any man, and to not more than one man in a century."

## The Head of the Party

"All free governments are managed by the combined wisdom and folly of the people." - Garfield

At the end of the war, Garfield supported the Radical Republican policies toward Reconstruction. He was a supporter of giving freed slaves the right to vote and was now willing to accept President Andrew Johnson's policy of conciliation towards the former states of the Confederacy and the rapid restoration of the Union. Thus, he advocated patience with the President's policies, but Garfield soured on Johnson by February 1866, when Lincoln's successor vetoed a bill extending the life of the Freedmen's Bureau. Garfield complained that Johnson was "crazy or drunk with opium."

While Garfield initially resisted the idea of impeaching President Johnson, by the time of Johnson's impeachment for violating the Tenure of Office Act in April 1868, he came out in support of it. Along with most Republicans, he was angered by the Senate's failure to vote to remove Johnson from office. However, in the wake of Ulysses S. Grant's election in 1868, Garfield moved away from the Radical Republicans, favoring the readmission of Georgia to the Union and opposing the passage of the Ku Klux Klan Act of 1871.

As Reconstruction continued in the South and Garfield's interest in it waned, he became increasingly focused on economic issues. He favored the gold standard throughout his political career, seeing the issuance of paper money not backed by gold during the Civil War (in the form of "greenbacks") as a wartime necessity only. Once placed on the Ways and Means Committee in the House in 1865, Garfield pressed his opposition to paper currency. In May 1868 he gave a long speech before the Committee that was later published. In it, he said, "I am aware that financial subjects are dull and univiting in comparison with those heroic themes which have absorbed the attention of Congress for the last five years. To turn from the consideration of armies and navies, victories and defeats, to the long array of figures which exhibit the debt, expenditure, taxation, and industry of the nation, requires no little courage and self-denial; but to those questions we must come, and to their solution Congress, political parties, and all thoughtful citizens must give their best efforts for many years to come."

He went on to advocate the resumption of payments in gold and silver, instead of the continued issuance of paper money that could not be redeemed for either. These questions of monetary policy would continue to occupy the country for the next several decades. Republicans almost universally advocated the gold standard, while Democrats were more divided on the issue, so Garfield's monetary views mirrored his party's.

However, Garfield differed with his party strongly over issues of trade. While Republicans favored protective tariffs to nurture domestic industries, Garfield was a strong advocate of lowering tariff rates and moving towards free trade. In a speech he delivered on July 10, 1866, he stated his position: "I hold that a properly-adjusted competition between home and foreign products is the best gunge by which to regulate international trade. Duties should be so high thai our manufacturers can fairly compete with the foreign product, but not so high as to enable them to drive out the foreign article, enjoy a monopoly of the trade, and regulate the price as they please. This is my doctrine of Protection. If Congress pursues this line steadily, we shall year by year approach more nearly to the basis of Free Trade, because we shall be more nearly able to compete with other nations on equal terms. I am' for Protection that leads to ultimate Free Trade. I am for that Free Trade which can only be achieved through a reasonable Protection."

On April 1, 1870, Garfield asserted his free trade stance more clearly: "I stand now where I have always stood since I have been a member of this House. I take the liberty of quoting, from the Congressional Globe of 1866, the following remarks which I then made on the subject of the tariff: 'We have seen that one extreme school of economists would place the price of all manufactured articles in the hands of foreign producers by rendering it impossible for our manufacturers to compete with them; while the other extreme school, by making it impossible for the foreigner to sell his competing wares in our market, would give the people no immediate check upon the prices which our manufacturers might fix for their products. I disagree with both these extremes. I hold that a properly adjusted competition between home and foreign products is the best gauge by which to regulate international trade. Duties should be so high that our manufacturers can fairly compete with the foreign product, but not so high as to enable them to drive out the foreign article, enjoy a monopoly of the trade, and regulate the price as they please. This is my doctrine of protection. If Congress pursues this line of policy steadily, we shall, year by your, approach more nearly to the basis of free-trade, because we shall be more nearly able to compete with other nations on equal terms. I am for a protection which leads to ultimate free-trade. I am for that free-trade which can only be achieved through a reasonable protection.' Mr. Chairman, examining thus the possibilities of the situation, I believe that the true course for the friends of protection to pursue is to reduce the rates on imports wherever we can justly and safely do so, and accepting neither of the extreme doctrines urged on this floor, endeavor to establish a stable policy that will commend itself to all patriotic and thoughtful people."

His tariff position did not make him popular in the party, and it eventually cost him his position on the Ways and Means Committee. The powerful newspaper publisher Horace Greeley was instrumental in keeping Garfield off the committee, but Garfield continued his interest in monetary matters through chairing the House Banking Committee. In this position he led the investigation of the Black Friday Gold Panic, which he blamed on the easy availability of paper money.

Corruption was a constant problem during Grant's presidency, and while Garfield was not enthusiastic about Grant's reelection in 1872, he could not avoid being caught up in one of the great scandals of the day. The Credit Mobilier scandal involved the offer of stock in the construction of the Transcontinental Railroad at below the market rate to Congressmen and Senators in return for guaranteeing additional appropriations to complete the project. News of the scandal broke in July 1872 during the political campaign and implicated several high-ranking Republican officeholders. One of them, Speaker of the House James G. Blaine, demanded the House investigate the scandal, and while the investigation exonerated Blaine, it revealed that Garfield had been offered 10 shares of stock, which he had refused. Garfield later admitted he received stock on credit, which he characterized as a loan, but Garfield's biographers have been unwilling to exonerate him in Crédit Mobilier. As Allan Peskin put it, "Did Garfield lie? Not exactly. Did he tell the truth? Not completely. Was he corrupted? Not really. Even Garfield's enemies never claimed that his involvement...influenced his behavior." Ira Rutkow wrote that "Garfield's real offense was that he knowingly denied to the House investigating committee that he had agreed to accept the stock and that he had also received a dividend of $329." R. G. Caldwell suggested that while Garfield "told the truth [before the committee], [he] certainly failed to tell the whole truth, clearly evading an answer to certain vital questions and thus giving the impression of worse faults than those of which he was guilty." The Credit Mobilier scandal, along with general voter dissatisfaction with Republican rule, led to the Republicans losing their majority in the House of Representatives in the election of 1874, but Garfield won reelection to his seat.

**Blaine**

With many of the Republican leaders defeated in the election, Garfield became the leader of the Republicans in the minority. The Democrats allowed Garfield to be a member of the Ways and Means committee, and he was viewed as a potential Speaker of the House when the Republicans regained power.

It was during his time in the minority that Garfield began to advocate against land grants to railroads. He also became a strong advocate for the establishment of the civil service to replace the practice of political appointments to fill positions in the government, which led to corruption.

In 1876, Garfield backed the candidacy of former Speaker Blaine at the Republican National Convention in Cincinnati that year, and when the convention nominated Ohio Governor Rutherford B. Hayes, Garfield supported him enthusiastically. He won re-election to his House seat in October, and when it appeared that the Democratic nominee Samuel Tilden won, the Republican governors of South Carolina, Louisiana, and Florida certified that Hayes had won their states in spite of vote totals that showed Tilden carried each one. As an observer in Louisiana, Garfield recommended that the entire vote of West Feliciana Parish, which had gone heavily to Tilden, be thrown out. Democrats were outraged, claiming that the Republicans were attempting to steal the election. In response, Congress established the Electoral Commission to determine the winner.

Over the objections of Democrats, Garfield was appointed to the Commission. The Commission eventually voted 8-7, along partisan lines, to award the presidency to Hayes, and Democrats agreed to accept the results in return for a promise from Hayes to remove the remaining federal troops from the South and end Reconstruction.

In the aftermath, Hayes relied on Garfield in the House to see his agenda passed, and in this position, he worked against the Bland-Allison Act that called for the government to issue silver coins as legal tender on par with gold.

With the support of Secretary of Treasury and former Ohio Senator John Sherman (the brother of Union General William Tecumseh Sherman), the Ohio General Assembly elected Garfield to an open Senate seat in January 1880. In return for his support, Garfield supported John Sherman in his quest for the Republican nomination for President in 1880. In addition to Sherman, favorites for the nomination included Blaine and former President Grant.

Despite his protests that he did not desire the office, Garfield was the favorite of a few Republicans, and one of the major disputes in the party was over civil service reform. A group called the Stalwarts supported the current system of political patronage to fill positions in the federal government and opposed the tentative moves towards a civil service that Hayes had made. The Half-Breeds supported civil service reform and succeeded in getting it put on the Republican Party's platform. One of the planks of the platform read, "The Republican party, adhering to the principles affirmed by its last National Convention of respect for the Constitutional rules governing appointment to office, adopts the declaration of President Hayes that the reform in the civil service shall be thorough, radical and complete. To that end it demands the co-operation of the Legislature with the Executive Departments of the Government, and that Congress shall so legislate that fitness, ascertained by proper practical tests, shall admit to the public service."

When the convention began, the leader of the Stalwarts, Senator Roscoe Conkling, proposed a rule that delegates pledge to support the eventual nominee. Three delegates from West Virginia refused, so Conkling proposed to have them expelled. Garfield rose to their defense. The *Associated Press* reported, "Mr. Garfield, of Ohio, who was received with a most flattering ovation, expressed his fear that the convention was about to commit a grave error. He would state the case. Every delegate save three had voted for a resolution, and the three who had voted against it had risen in their places and stated they expected and intended to support the nominee of the convention. But it was not, in their judgment, a wise thing at this time to pass the resolution which all the rest of the delegates had voted for. Were they to be disfranchised because they thought so? [Cries of 'No! No!'] That was the question. Was every delegate to have his Republicanism inquired into before he was allowed to vote? Delegates were responsible for their votes, not to the convention, but to their constituents. He himself would never, in any convention, vote against his judgment. He regretted that the gentlemen from West Virginia had thought it best to break the harmony of the convention by their dissent. He did not know those gentlemen, nor their affiliations, nor their relations to the candidates. If this convention expelled these men, then the convention would have to purge itself at the end of every vote and inquire how many delegates who had voted "no" should go out. He trusted that the gentleman from New York would withdraw his resolution and let the convention proceed with its business. [Loud cheering.]"

In the face of opposition, Conkling withdrew his resolution and Garfield's stock rose in the eyes of many delegates.

On the evening of the fourth day of the Convention, a call was made for names to be entered into nomination. Blaine was placed in nomination, as was Grant (by Senator Conkling). Garfield rose in the Ohio delegation and entered John Sherman into nomination, stating, "The great fiscal affairs of the nation and the great business interests of the country he has guarded and pre served, while executing the law of resumption, and effecting its object, without a jar, and against the false prophecies of one-half of the press and all the Democracy of this continent. He has shown himself able to meet with calmness the great emergencies of the Government for twenty- five years. He has trodden the perilous heights of public duty, and against all the shafts of malice has borne his breast unharmed. He has stood in the blaze of 'that fierce light that beats against the throne," but its fiercest ray has found no flaw in his armor, no stain on his shield.' I do not present him as a better Republican, or as a better man than thousands of others we honor, but I present him for your deliberate consideration. I nominate John Sherman, of Ohio."

The roll call for the nomination began on the morning of June 6, 1880. The delegates voted for 18 ballots in the morning, and on the 18th ballot, Garfield, whose name had not been entered in nomination the evening before, received two votes. The Convention adjourned that evening after the 28th ballot, and the voting continued the next day. On the 34th ballot, Wisconsin gave 16 votes to Garfield, and on the 35th ballot, he received 50 votes. The 36th ballot had the delegates other than those for Grant go for Garfield, giving him 399 votes and the nomination. An eyewitness later reported, "After the excitement had subsided there was a sort of love-feast, Mr. Conkling rose and moved that the name of James A. Garfield be unanimously presented as the nominee of the Convention, and said: 'I trust that the zeal, the fervor, and now the unanimity of the scenes of the Convention will be transplanted to the fields of the country, and that all of us who have borne a part against each other will be found, with equal zeal, bearing the banners and carrying the lances of the Republican party into the ranks of the enemy.' General Logan said: 'Whatever may have transpired in this Convention that may have produced feelings of annoyance will be, I hope, considered as a matter of the past. I, with the friends of one of the grandest men on the face of the earth, stood here to fight a friendly battle for his nomination, but this Convention has chosen another leader, and the men who stood by Grant will be seen in the front of the contest for Mr. Garfield…As one of the Republicans from Illinois, I second the nomination of James A. Garfield, and hope it will be made unanimous.' It was done."

**A cartoon depicting Grant surrendering the nomination to Garfield**

That afternoon, Chester A. Arthur of New York was nominated as the Republican candidate for Vice President, in large part to placate the Stalwart faction of the party.

In accepting the nomination, Garfield told a delegation of delegates, "I assure you that the information you have officially given me brings the sense of very grave responsibility, and especially so in view of the fact that I was a member of your body, a fact which could not have been so with propriety had I had the slightest expectation that my own name would be connected with the nomination for the office. I have felt with you great solicitude regarding the situation of our party during the struggle, but believing that you are correct in assuring me that substantial unity has been reached in the conclusion, it gives me gratification far greater than any personal pleasure your announcement can bring. I accept the trust committed to my hands. As to the work of our party, as to the character of the campaign to be entered upon, I will take an early occasion to reply more fully than I can properly do now. I thank you for the assurances of confidence and esteem and unity which you have presented me with, and shall hope that we may see our future as promising as are the indications of to-night."

Garfield's nomination was enthusiastically received by Republicans. President Hayes telegraphed, "You will receive no heartier congratulation to-day than mine; this both for your own and your country's sake." Sherman, for his part, was magnanimous, writing "I congratulate you with all my heart upon your nomination as President of the United States. You have saved the Republican party and the country from a great peril and assured the continued success of Republican principles."

**A campaign poster**

Facing Garfield in the 1880 presidential election was the Democratic candidate, Major General Winfield Scott Hancock, one of the prominent heroes of Gettysburg. There were tensions among Republicans between Stalwarts and Half-Breeds, but Garfield was able to persuade the Stalwarts to set aside their differences and unite for the election.

By 1880, the South was solidly in Democratic hands, and much of the North was expected to back Garfield and the Republicans, so the contest was likely to be settled by a couple of close swing states, including New York and Indiana. Republicans emphasized the tariff as a major issue, criticizing the Democratic platform's call for tariff reform as potentially damaging Northern workers. When the votes were cast, only 2,000 votes out of 9.2 million cast separated the two, but Garfield won easily in the Electoral College, 214-155.

After his election, Garfield spent time trying to balance the Stalwart and Half-Breed factions among the Republicans. Thanks to Blaine's role in getting Garfield the nomination, Garfield named him Secretary of State. He populated his Cabinet with representatives of both factions, which still did not prevent infighting, particularly Blaine's opposition to Garfield's nomination of his adversary, Wayne MacVeagh, as Attorney General. Similarly, Conkling was infuriated by Garfield's nomination of Thomas Lemuel James as Attorney General, leading to a feud between the Senator and the President that culminated with Garfield's nomination of Judge William H. Robertson, a political enemy of Conkling, to be Collector of Customs for the Port of New York, which at the time was a prize patronage position. When he failed to defeat the nomination in the Senate, Conkling resigned along with New York's other Senator, Thomas C. Platt, in a gambit to have their position solidified by being re-elected to their seats. The New York Legislature failed to oblige, Robertson was confirmed at collector, and Garfield had a clear victory over the Stalwarts.

The initial months of Garfield's administration emphasized reform of the civil service first advocated by Hayes, but it otherwise departed little from other administrations in the exercise of executive power. In his inaugural address, he voiced continued support for preserving the right to vote among African-Americans and opposition to the Mormon practice of polygamy. He said of civil service reform, "The civil service can never be placed on a satisfactory basis until it is regulated by law. For the good of the service itself, for the protection of those who are entrusted with the appointing power against the waste of time and obstruction of the public business caused by the inordinate pressure for place, and for the protection of incumbents against intrigue and wrong, I shall at the proper time ask Congress to fix the tenure of the minor offices vf the several executive departments and prescribe the grounds upon which removals shall be made during terms for which incumbents have been appointed."

He also outlined his philosophy of the executive: "Finally, acting always within the authority and limitations of the Constitution, invading neither the rights of the States nor the reserved rights of the people, it will be the purpose of my administration to maintain the authority of the nation, and in all places within its jurisdiction to enforce obedience to all the laws of the Union in the interests of the people; to demand rigid economy in all the expenditures of the Government, and to require the honest and faithful service of all executive officers, remembering that the offices were created, not for the benefit of the incumbents or their supporters, but for the service of the Government."

He did advocate a universal system of education, funded by the federal government, to help African-Americans secure their rights, but none of Garfield's proposals would come to pass for fateful reasons.

**The Assassination**

"If wrinkles must be written upon our brows, let them not be written upon the heart. The spirit should not grow old."

July 2, 1881 began like any other day in post-Civil War America. Independence Day was approaching, and with it a series of parades, political speeches and town picnics. Garfield, inaugurated as president of the United States just a few months earlier, was looking forward to an enjoyable time that day speaking at his own alma mater, Williams College, and getting away from the heat of Washington for a few days. As it turned out, however, Garfield would never give the speech he had prepared, nor would he ever enjoy any of the festivities planned for the holiday. In fact, he would never make it to catch the 9:30 a.m. train he was scheduled to take before Charles Julius Guiteau stepped in his way and shot him twice.

**Pictures of Guiteau**

After such a heinous crime takes place, people often claim the accused seemed normal, but no one who knew him would ever say that about Guiteau. He was born in 1841 to a severely mentally ill mother and a father overwhelmed by his wife's behavior. After his mother died in 1848, Guiteau's father turned him over to his older sister Franky to raise while he worked and tried to find another wife. Later, when the elder Guiteau did remarry, his new wife found it difficult to deal with the boy, who could neither speak plainly nor keep still for more than a few seconds at a time.

By the time he was in his mid-20s, Guiteau had found an outlet for his personality in religious fanaticism, which had him traveling the country preaching and writing books primarily concerned with the end times. He was also a moderately successful con-man who typically left each town with a trail of debt behind him. He later told the judge in his trial, "I will tell you how I do it, Judge, and perhaps you can learn if you want to borrow money. … I come right out square with a friend. I do not lie and sneak and do that kind of business, or anything. I say, 'I want to get $25; I want to use a little money;' and the probability is that if he has got the money about him, he will pull the money right out and give it to me. That is the way I get my money. I take it and thank him and go about my business. …  If a man has the money, he gives it to me on a sudden impulse, I suppose; and if he has not, that settles it."

When the religious obsession waned or he failed at his most current pursuit, he took on a new passion: politics. Guiteau found fertile ground for his interest during the 1880 Republican primaries by becoming a part of the Stalwart faction, which was determined to see Ulysses Grant nominated for a third term. Opposing them were the Half-Breeds, a group backing James Blaine of Maine. In the end, neither faction mustered enough votes to win, which resulted in a compromise candidate, James Garfield, being nominated.

Guiteau seemed satisfied when Garfield chose Stalwart Chester Arthur to be his running mate. He often volunteered at the Republican headquarters in New York City. He often asked to be allowed to speak at public functions but was allowed to only once, to a small group of barely franchised African-American voters.

**Garfield/Arthur campaign placard.** *Currier & Ives*

**Arthur**

Unfortunately, when Garfield won the general election, Guiteau's diseased mind believed that it was largely due to his speech. He immediately began to write to the president-elect, informing him of his good works and asking for a political appointment, and in the weeks following Garfield's March inauguration, Guiteau became even more demanding, insisting that he deserved a diplomatic post somewhere overseas. After requesting a position in Vienna, Guiteau asked for one in Paris. By the middle of May, Blaine, whom Garfield had made his Secretary of State, had had enough and told Guiteau on the 14th, "Never bother me again about the Paris consulship so long as you live."

**Blaine**

Despondent, Guiteau focused his rage and disappointment on Garfield, concluding that the only way to make things right was to remove the man he felt he had put in office from the White House. Indeed, he came to believe that he was under divine direction to do so.

By the middle of June, Guiteau had formulated a plan, so he borrowed $15 with which to purchase a .45 caliber snub-nosed revolver. It was later asserted that Guiteau bought that kind of gun because it would look good in a museum following his historic act.

**Guiteau's Pistol. Drawing by James Dabney McCabe**

**A picture of the pistol, now housed at the Smithsonian**

Regardless of whether that's true, he was certainly intent on taking action, and the following day, June 16, he began writing an "Address to the American People," which seemed to have fully set forth his views: "I conceived the idea of removing the president four weeks ago. Not a soul knew of my purpose. I conceived the idea myself and kept it to myself. I read the newspapers carefully, for and against the administration, and gradually the conviction dawned on me that the president's removal was a political necessity, because he proved a traitor to the men that made him, and thereby imperiled the life of the republic. ... Ingratitude is the basest of crimes. That the president, under the manipulation of his secretary of state, has been guilty of the basest ingratitude to the stalwarts, admits of no denial. The expressed purpose of the president has been to crush Gen. Grant and Senator Conkling, and thereby open the way for his renomination in 1884. In the president's madness he has wrecked the once grand old Republican Party, and for this he dies. ... This is not murder. It is a political necessity. It will make my friend Arthur president, and save the republic. ... I leave my justification to God and the American people."

When asked during his trial about his rationale for killing Garfield, Guiteau replied, "I would not have accepted the Paris consulship, if the President had urged it and Mr. Blaine had urged it upon me with the utmost determination, any time after the 1st of June. ... I would not have done it, because my mind was fully fixed as to the necessity of the President's removal for the good of the American people. I would not have taken the Paris consulship at any time after the 1st of June. ... I would have sent it right back any time after the 1st of June. My whole heart and mind and inspiration was in removing him. ... If General Garfield had had the proper respect for [my] letters, things would have been very different today. But what did he do but sell himself, soul and body, to Mr. Blaine. ...he did not appreciate the sentiment and kindness of those letters, but put himself into Mr. Blaine's hands, and allowed Mr. Blaine to use the Presidency to crush Grant and Conkling, and the very men that made him."

WHITE HOUSE
PRESIDENTS BELL
BULL DOG
ENGLISH
AN OFFICE OR YOUR LIFE!
WAC.

**Political cartoons depicting Guiteau in the wake of the shooting**

Once Guiteau had made up his mind to kill Garfield and had armed himself, he merely had to find an opportune moment in which to commit the deed. In late June, he actually followed Garfield's carriage from the White House to Blaine's home, but he decided at the last minute not to attempt to kill the president that time. On another occasion, he followed the President to a railway station, thinking that would be the perfect place in which to shoot him, but according to one source, he was deterred by the presence of Garfield's wife. "[T]he affectionate husband lifted his wife from the carriage, and Guiteau saw her thin hands and pale, sweet face, he was defeated again; and, stuffing his revolver in his pocket, said, 'I'll wait till she is better.'" Although he tarried in those instances, Guiteau made careful plans to avoid being carried off and killed by the angry mob that would no doubt form upon Garfield's death, for he believed that if he made it safely to the jail, those who agreed with him politically would no doubt arrange his release.

   Then, on June 30, the local newspaper reported that Garfield would be taking the 9:30 train out of the Baltimore and Potomac Station, bound for Williams College in Massachusetts, on July 2. Guiteau arose early that morning, took his new gun, and went down to a secluded river bank near his home, where he practiced his aim until he was sure that he could hit his intended target. After that, Guiteau proceeded to the train station to await his victim.

**Baltimore & Potomac Terminal. National Gallery of Art.**

   Once he reached the station, Guiteau took up his post in the Ladies Sitting Room, which the president would have to pass to reach his own train. A woman named Mrs. White was in charge of the Room that day and described the shooting: "I had noticed this man Guiteau lounging around the ladies' room for a half hour before the arrival of the' President. I did not like his appearance from the first time I saw him. It is my business to see that such characters do not loaf around the ladies' room, and I thought seriously of having him pointed out to our watchman, Mr. Scott, so that he should be made [to] stay in the gentlemen's room. When the President and Secretary Blaine entered he was standing near the entrance door. He wheeled to the left and fired, evidently aiming for the heart. It was a quick shot and struck the President in the left arm.

The President did not at first seem to realize that he had been struck, although Secretary Blaine instantly stepped to one side as though dazed at this unexpected movement. The President then partly turned around and the assassin advancing two steps fired the second time — the whole thing being the work of a few moments. The President advanced one step, then fell to the floor. I ran to him at once and raised his head and held it in that position until some gentlemen came, and we remained until his son came from the car where he was seated, with the rest of the Presidential party, awaiting the arrival of his father."

**The *Associated Press'* depiction of Guiteau shooting Garfield**

According to other witnesses, after shooting Garfield, Guiteau calmly wiped his pistol clean and put it in his pocket. He then turned to leave, having ordered a cab to take him directly to the jail.

Police officer Patrick Kearney may have been the last person to speak to Garfield before he was shot. He recalled, "I thought that that was a peculiar thing, but before I could follow it up closer I saw the President's party driving down Sixth Street to the depot, and I had to go and look after them. They drove to the B Street entrance. Secretary Blaine was with the President, and the two entered the depot together. The President walked up to me, and asked how much time he had before the train left. It was twenty minutes after nine o'clock I saw by looking at my watch, and I told the President that he had ten minutes. Just as he thanked me I heard a pistol shot, and turning, I saw the man that I had been watching previously standing about ten feet away, in the shadow of the main entrance to the waiting-room, levelling his pistol across his arm. He fired a second shot before I could speak to him, and darted between myself and the President and Secretary Blaine into the street. The President reeled and fell just in front of me. As he fell he said something I could not exactly understand, and Secretary Blaine, with a terrified look, pushed towards him, exclaiming, 'My God, he has been murdered! What is the meaning of this?' 'In God's name, man,' I shouted, ' what did you shoot the President for?'"

**The Illustrated Newspaper's depiction of Garfield just after being shot**

Mr. Parks, who worked at the train station, witnessed the shooting and remembered, "I had been watching for the arrival of the President through the small window between my office and the ladies' waiting room, and saw this man Guiteau, who was a small man, slight in physique, with short pointed beard on his chin. His movements were those of an uneasy, nervous man. At that time there were but few persons present, and nearly all ladies. I was attracted by the report of a pistol. I immediately peered into the ladies' room and saw the assassin, pistol in hand, standing about two feet inside of the entrance door. I saw him advance two paces and fire the second shot. … There was an interval of about four seconds between the first and second shots. Just as soon as the second shot was fired I took in the situation, and ran out of the office for the purpose of securing the assassin. In the meantime Guiteau tried to make his escape by the main door on

Sixth Street, but being headed off he turned to make away by the exit of the ladies' room on C Street, when I grappled him by the left hand and the left shoulder, and held him until Officer Kearney and Depot Watchman Scott came to my assistance in a few moments, the former holding him by the right shoulder and the latter securing him by his clothing in the back. He said that this letter which he held in his hand and flourished frantically about his head was going to General [William Tecumseh] Sherman and explained all. When I first laid my hand on him he made desperate efforts to release himself, but upon finding that it was useless he subsided."

In fact, the letter the Guiteau had in his hand, which he apparently dropped as he was being hauled away, read, "I have just shot the President.  I shot him several times as I wished him to go as easily as possible. His death was a political necessity. I am a lawyer, theologian, and politician. I am a Stalwart of the Stalwarts. I was with General Grant and the rest of our men, in New York during the canvass. I am going to the Jail. Please order out your troops, and take possession of the jail at once." Naturally, when General William Sherman heard about the shooting and the letter, he stated emphatically, "I don't know the writer, never heard of or saw him to my knowledge, and hereby return it to the keeping of the above-named parties as testimony in the case."

As the crowd began to cry out that Guiteau be lynched, Kearney got him out the door and to a nearby police station. All the while, Guiteau was calmly reassuring those around him, "It is all right, it is all right. I am a Stalwart."

Still lying on the Ladies' Room floor wounded, Garfield's head was cradled in Mrs. White's lap, and she held him gently, crying throughout the ordeal as he began to vomit and go into shock. Reporter James Young managed to get into the room and later wrote, "The first person I saw was Secretary Windom. He was standing alone, as pale as death, and the tears were trickling down his cheeks. Knowing him well I said : 'Mr. Secretary, where is the President, and what does this mean?' He replied, 'There he lies in yonder corner in that group. It is as much of a mystery to me as it is to you.' I moved over about two yards, and there I saw the President lying on a mattress which had been hastily brought from the sleeping apartments of one of the depot employees. There were probably thirty people around him, many of whom were women, who had been waiting for the southern trains. Secretary Blaine had hold of one of the President's hands, and Postmaster-General James was assisting to get him into a sitting posture. His face showed a deathly paleness, and he had a look of surprise, as if caused by pain and despair. He was vomiting and seemed to have no control of himself. His coat and vest had been ripped from him and his trousers loosened. The matter he had vomited had fallen on his shirt below the bosom, which made it seem as if the ball of the assassin had penetrated the intestines."

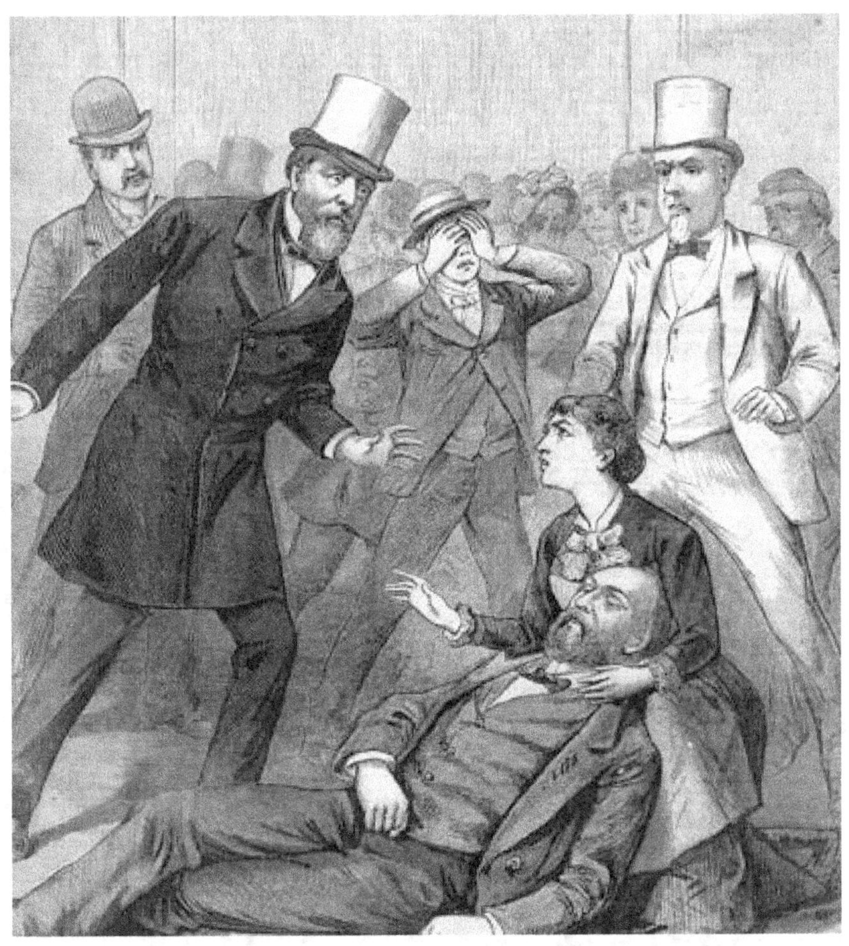

**A depiction of Garfield being held by Mrs. White**

Tragically, two of Garfield's sons, James and Harry, were also with him that day. Mrs. White remembered, "When I ran to him he was deathly pale, but perfectly conscious. In about two or three minutes he vomited. His son was kneeling beside him at this time. He asked me if I saw who shot his father, and I replied, ' Yes, and he is caught.' He said somebody would have to pay for this. The young man and I thought the President was dying, so pale was he. He tried to raise his head and get his hand on the wound near the thigh, but he was too weak to do so. I noticed Guiteau at the depot either early this week or the latter part of last."

**A picture of Garfield's children, with James and Harry standing**

Young also observed this scene: "Near him was his son, a lad of sixteen. Poor boy, he was almost beside himself. He wrung his hands and cried in a piteous manner. With him were the son of Colonel Rockwell, and Secretary Hunt, who, in every way natural to human beings, were trying to comfort him."

Of course, the comfort of the family would have to take a backseat to caring for the injured president. Young continued, "In less than ten minutes Secretary Blaine gave orders to have the President removed to the upper floor of the depot, to the officers' room, where there would be plenty of air and a freedom from the mob which was rapidly gathering. Colonel Rockwell and Adjutant-General Corbin soon made a passage way, and the President was borne by a number of the colored porters of the depot to the upper floor. I waited down-stairs, and in about half an hour he was carried down, placed in an ambulance, and under a strong guard of mounted police was driven to the White House. I immediately left the depot and hurriedly went up Pennsylvania Avenue. Although it was not an hour since the shooting took place, I found the avenue crowded with people, some standing in groups, regardless of the broiling hot sun, discussing the event, others hurrying towards the depot, and others pushing and rushing and wending their way no one knows where."

**Rockwell**

Dr. Smith Townshend, the local District Health Officer, was the first doctor to reach the fallen President. He recalled, "I arrived at the depot four minutes after he was shot, and found him lying upon the floor of the depot, surrounded by an immense gathering. He was then in a fainting condition. From his appearance and the pulsations at the wrist I thought he was dying. I took some of the pillows from under his head that he might rest easier. I prescribed aromatic spirits of ammonia and brandy, which revived him. I ordered the police to get the crowd back, and had the President removed to an upper room. He rallied considerably, and I proceeded to examine his wounds. I found that the last bullet had entered his back about two and a half inches to the right of the vertebrae. When I placed my finger in the wound some hemorrhage followed. I then administered another dose of the stimulant, which again revived him. In the meantime Drs. Purvis and Bliss arrived. I had, however, previously asked him how he felt and where the most pain was felt, and he answered in his right leg and feet. I asked him the character of his pain, and he said that it was a pricking sensation. Dr. Woodward, of the army, also came in afterwards, and after a consultation we concluded to remove him to the White House. It was then about ten o'clock, and all the members of the Cabinet were present. …after I made the examination of the wounds the President looked up and asked me what I thought of it. I answered that I did not consider it serious. He continued, 'I thank you, doctor, but I am a dead man.'"

Soon, there were 10 other doctors from around the city, and they ordered mattresses pulled out of nearby sleeper cars and put in the back of an express wagon. The President was placed on board and driven carefully back to the White House, where he was placed in his own bed. Townshend continued, "When we arrived at the White House, and just before he was removed from the ambulance, he asked me to call to Major Brock to clear the hall, as there might be another assassin around. Quite a number of the doctors and others went along with the ambulance. When taken from the ambulance he was in a fainting condition, and we revived him with stimulants, and upon consultation we concluded to give a hypodermic injection of morphia and allow him to rest until three o'clock. Afterwards we gave him an injection of atropia and morphia, which brought his pulse up to eighty. At three o'clock, when we had another consultation, we found his pulse 102 and temperature 96, or two and a half below normal. While we were in consultation he became very much nauseated and vomited considerably. Upon examining the wound we found much dulness and tension of the right hypogastric region, restlessness and pain, which indicated internal hemorrhage. We immediately gave him one hypodermic injection of a quarter of a grain of morphia, which relieved him of the pain and quieted him. At half-past four o'clock this afternoon, when I left him, he was in a partially comatose state and unconscious. He was not talking much, but answered some of our questions."

**An illustration depicting doctors discussing Garfield's condition.**

Some of the doctors who examined him more closely had few encouraging words for him. One said aloud, "He is dying. Look at his eyes; they are becoming fixed."Another one asked, "Why don't we do something?" Needless to say, this did not bolster the president's morale, and it was left to his wife Lucretia, who arrived and lifted his spirits by telling him, "Well, my dear, you are not going to die as I am here to nurse you back to life; so please do not speak again of death."

On July 5, Blaine's wife wrote to one of their children, "Maggie, nurse, came running into the room crying, 'They have telephoned over to you, Mrs. Blaine, that the President is assassinated.' Emmons flew, for we all remembered, with one accord, that his father was with him. By the time I had reached the door, I saw that it must be true — everybody on the street, and wild. Mrs. Sherman got a carriage and drove over to the White House. Found the streets in front jammed and the doors closed, but they let us through and in. The President still at the station, so drove thitherward. Met the mounted police clearing the avenue, then the ambulance, turned and followed into that very gateway where, on the 4th of March, we had watched him enter. I stood with Mrs. MacVeagh in the hall, when a dozen men bore him above their heads, stretched on a mattress, and as he saw us and held us with his eye, he kissed his hand to us — I thought I should die: and when they brought him into his chamber and had laid him on the bed, he turned his eyes to me, beckoned, and when I went to him, pulled me down, kissed me again and again and said, 'Whatever happens, I want you to promise to look out for Crete,' — the name he always gives his wife…'Don't leave me until Crete comes.' I took my old bonnet off and just stayed…At six, or thereabouts, Mrs. Garfield came, frail, fatigued, desperate, but firm and quiet and full of purpose to save, and I think now there is a possibility of succeeding."

In doing so, Mrs. Blaine soon became a witness to history. She described the events of the following day: "After breakfast I went with your father to the White House, and finding that their arrangements for nursing were all made for the day, I came immediately away. It looks as though Mr. Garfield would live. He is now, six o'clock, still comfortable and has asked for beefsteak. They will not, of course, let him have it. Mrs. Sherman and Tom were there, who came to let the President and Mrs. Garfield know that yesterday the men of his order made their communion an offering for the President's recovery. Your father has stayed in and read and signed dispatches and received callers, and now W. and your father have gone to the White House to make inquiries and thence to pay their daily visit to V.P. Arthur, who is on Capitol Hill…When I was with the President yesterday, as I was all the forenoon, he looked up at me and said, 'When I am ready to eat, I am going to break into Mrs. Blaine's larder.'"

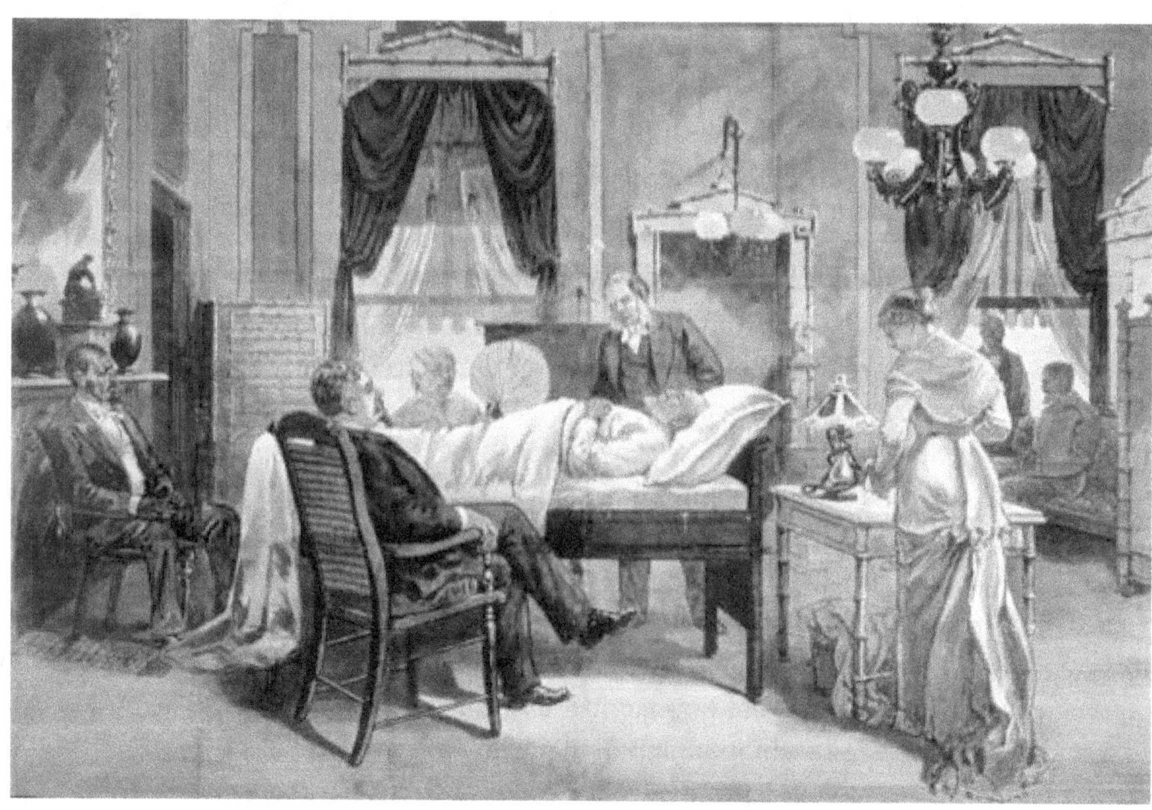

**_Harper's Weekly_ illustration of Garfield convalescing in bed**

With his family gathered around him, Garfield slept through the first night, disturbed only by periodic bouts of vomiting, and the next morning, he had full bowel and urination function, as well as a normal temperature and strong pulse. With these signs that there was no organ damage, the doctors began to feel more optimistic, and on July 8, Mrs. Blaine could write to her kids, "Everything seems to be going as well with the President as the most loving heart can wish. … No danger now, no anxiety about paralysis, or bullet in the liver, and every prospect of a speedy recovery in all his parts. … I have been to the White House this morning, but saw none but officials. Left your father there in consultation with the doctors. … I suppose you have noticed that the President came here Friday afternoon. … Now it seems this Guiteau followed him to this house, waited to shoot him on his return, but not wanting to hurt Secretary Blaine, had to give it up that time."

As the days went by, it seemed increasingly likely that the president might indeed survive his wounds, and by mid-July, Blaine himself wrote, "Garfield, I think, is surely destined to be much more speedily well and out than is generally thought. I differ from the doctors about the direction of the ball — have never believed that the liver was pierced at all — and think the event will prove that I am right." After another week passed, Mrs. Blaine wrote, "Your father saw the President for six minutes yesterday morning, the first time since that fateful Saturday. They had put him…off day after day, till he would be denied no longer. He looked better than your father expected to see him, though his voice was weak. Mrs. Garfield told me yesterday, she considered him out of danger. Isn't it wonderfully good?"

Of course, the president was far from out of the woods, and the very next day, July 23, Mrs. Blaine reported, "I am just home from the White House…Every one looking very anxious and sober. Mrs. Garfield said the President did not mind much who was in the room with him today." A few days later, on July 29, Garfield met briefly with his Cabinet, the only such meeting held following the shooting.

During his trial, Guiteau would tell the court that "the Deity allowed the Doctors to finish my work gradually," and he was probably correct. Had the doctors left the bullet in place and just kept the wound bandaged and clean, Garfield would almost certainly have survived and had a full recovery. However, in their efforts to locate the bullet, they frequently used dirty fingers or instruments, which introduced infections into Garfield's system that drove his fever up and his appetite down. In the 11 weeks that he lingered following the shooting, the president wasted away before their very eyes, going from 200 pounds to just 135 pounds.

As the heat in Washington reached its height, Navy engineers placed fans in the president's room and kept them blowing over large boxes of ice to help keep him cool, and Alexander Graham Bell created a metal detector that would have located the bullet had the president not been lying on a metal bed frame when it was used. However, nothing could stop the infections, which spread and brought on blood poisoning that caused the stricken president to hallucinate and suffer from infected abscesses that broke out all over his body. On August 23, Mrs. Blaine wrote, "I was at the White House last night. Miss Edson abandoned hope. Why, indeed, should that angel tarry longer by that bed when the poor sufferer has lost his own identity, praying to have that other man taken from him away, and to be relieved from that other man's face which cleaves to and drags upon his? About ten, or perhaps later, we came home, when your father penned his bulletin to Lowell." Two days later, she added, "I suppose you can see as well as another that hope is over. Every night I try to brace for that telephone which I am sure before morning will send its shrill summons. The morning is a little reassuring, for light of itself gives courage. Your father I follow upstairs and down like a dog."

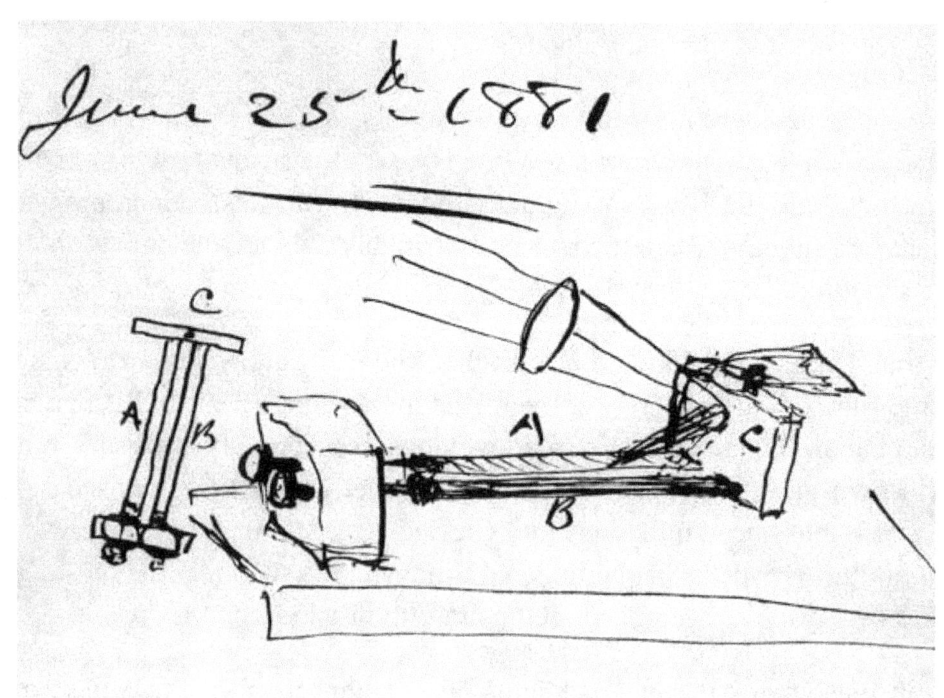


**A sketch of Bell's metal detector.**

By this time, many began wondering if there was anything that could be done to save the nation's leader. William Chandler, who subsequently became Secretary of the Navy, wrote on August 29, "I have no patience with the fault-finders, and I think Dr. … ought to be suppressed; but I wish the doctors had found out before six weeks had passed where the ball went, and had kept opium out of him, which, combined with the extreme heat of Washington, is likely to prevent his recovery just as it seems evident that he might recover from the direct influence of the ball…. I do not feel as if I ever wanted to set foot in its streets again. I expect to see its effect in the changed looks and gray hairs of my friends who have been there during these anxious weeks."

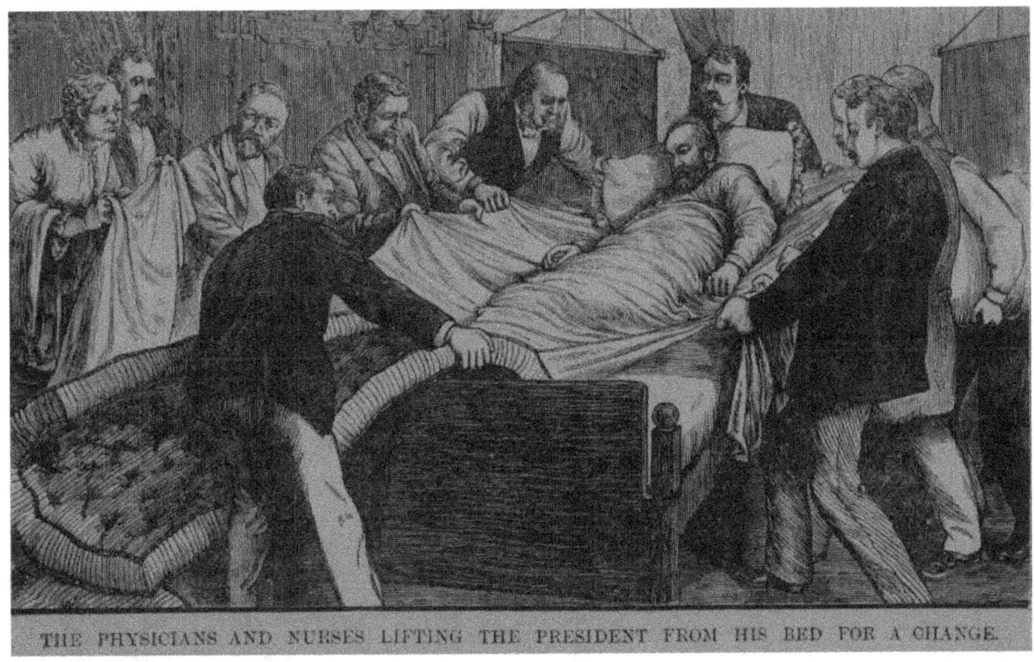


**An illustration depicting Garfield being cared for by nurses and doctors**

Finally, on September 6, the doctors decided to allow Garfield to travel with his family to the Jersey Shore, hoping that the cool sea air might help turn the tide in his recovery. Blaine noted, "President left this morning at 6 o'clock. We follow in an hour. I tremble for the experiment and its success, but it was fatal to stay here…" Later, he added, "The President holds his own. I wish I could say a great deal more, but I cannot, and I am overcome with dread of the final result. He is so greatly reduced; still, he has lived out seventy-one days, and that is a great thing. Was there ever a life so desired and so prayed for! May God look down in mercy!"

Sadly, Blaine's prayers, and those of the nation, would not be answered, at least not in the way they intended. While Garfield rested and enjoyed the cool days at the shore, the infection continued to spread, leading ultimately to blood poisoning, pneumonia and, finally, a burst aneurism that ended his life on September 19, 1881, 80 days after he was shot.

An autopsy was performed the following day, and the report read in part, "It was found that the ball, after fracturing the right eleventh rib, had passed through the spinal column in front of the spinal cord, fracturing the body of the first lumbar vertebra, driving a number of small fragments of bone into the adjacent soft parts, and lodging below the pancreas, about two inches and a half to the left of the spine, and behind the peritoneum, where it had become completely encysted. The immediate cause of death was secondary hemorrhage from one of the mesenteric arteries adjoining the track of the ball, the blood rupturing the peritoneum, and nearly a pint escaping into the abdominal cavity. This hemorrhage is believed to have been the cause of the severe pain in the lower part of the chest complained of just before death. An abscess-cavity, six inches by four in dimensions, was found in the vicinity of the gall-bladder, between the liver and the transverse colon, which were strongly adherent. It did not involve the substance of the liver, and no communication was found between it and the wound. A long, suppurating channel extended from the external wound, between the loin muscles and the right kidney almost to the right groin. This channel, now known to be due to the burrowing of pus from the wound, was supposed, during life, to have been the track of the ball."

In the end, the wound itself was not the ultimate cause of death. The autopsy report explained, "On an examination of the organs of the chest evidences of severe bronchitis were found on both sides, with broncho-pneumonia of the lower portions of the right lung, and, though to a much less extent, of the left. … In reviewing the history of the case in connection with the autopsy, it is quite evident that the different suppurating surfaces, and especially the fractured spongy tissue of the vertebrae, furnish a sufficient explanation of the septic condition which existed."

**A picture of Garfield's casket lying in the Capitol rotunda**

**An illustration depicting mourners viewing the body**

An illustration depicting Garfield's funeral back in Ohio

A contemporary mourning ribbon

**Commemorative sheet music for Garfield's funeral**

## The Aftermath

"Meanwhile, the assassin, almost boasting of his crime and waiting for the death, eagerly inquired every day for the news. He declared that it was for the good of the nation that he committed the deed, and pretended to pray for the people. His prison was guarded by police and soldiers to protect him from the mob, for the people regarded him and his act in almost a frenzy of rage. Even one of the sentinels set to guard him attempted to shoot him, and but for the bar of iron on his cell would have succeeded. The ball grazed Guiteau's head. That unlawful attempt on his life tended to make the murderer change his demeanor, and from that time on the fear of death was so great that every footstep in the corridor startled him, and when told that the President was dying his seared conscience assumed again its sceptre, and made him crouch and cower, and call on God and man for mercy." – Russell H. Conwell, *The Life, Speeches, and Public Services of James A. Garfield, Twentieth President of the United States* (1881)

**An illustration depicting Guiteau's arraignment in *A Complete History of the Trial of Charles Guiteau***

In the aftermath of the shooting, the police had taken Guiteau into custody and began trying to make some sense of what he had done, but understandably, this proved to be challenging because Guiteau was unlike anyone else they had ever dealt with. Lieutenant' Eckloff of the Metropolitan Police Headquarters recalled, "When he was brought in we searched him, but he took from his pocket unassisted the pistol that he had used. It was too large for the hip pocket, and he had considerable difficulty in getting it out. He said to us that we need not be excited at all, that if we wanted to know why he did the act we would find it in his papers in the breast pocket of his coat. We took the pistol out of his hand and found it to be a five-shooter, with two barrels empty. It was what is termed an ' English bull-dog,' and carries a ball as large as a navy revolver does."

Detective McElfresh interviewed the suspect on their way to the jail and relayed that their exchange was something along these lines;

McElfresh: "Where are you from ?"

Guiteau: "I am a native-born American; born in Chicago."

McElfresh: "Why did you do this ?"

Guiteau: "I did it to save the Republican party."

McElfresh: "What is your politics?"

Guiteau: "I am a stalwart among the stalwarts. With Garfield out of the way we can carry all the Northern States, and with him in the way we can't carry a single one. Who are you?"

McElfresh: "A detective officer of this department."

Guiteau: "You stick to me and have me put in the third story front at the jail. General Sherman is coming down to take charge. Arthur and all these men are my friends, and I'll have you made Chief of Police. When you get back to the police you will find that I left two bundles of papers at the news stand, which will explain all."

McElfresh: "Is there anybody else with you in this matter?"

Guiteau: "Not a living soul; I contemplated this thing for the last few weeks."

When the men finally arrived at the jail, Guiteau admitted he had been there before: "I was down here last Saturday morning and wanted them to let me look through, and they told me that I could not, but to come on Monday. I wanted, to see what kind of quarters I would have to occupy."

**A contemporary depiction of the jail where Guiteau was kept**

**A modern picture of the jail**

When the police searched Guiteau, they discovered the letter he had been carrying in his pocket, and it read in part, "July 2, 1881. To the White House: The President's tragic death was a sad necessity, but it will unite the Republican Party and save the Republic. Life is a flimsy dream, and it matters little when one goes; a human life is of small value. During the war thousands of brave boys went down without a tear. I presume the President was a Christian, and that he will be happier in Paradise than here. It will be no worse for Mrs. Garfield, dear soul, to part with her husband this way than by natural death. He is liable to go at any time, anyway. I had no ill-will towards the President. His death was a political necessity. I am a lawyer, a theologian, and a politician…I have some papers for the press, which I shall leave with Byron Andrews and his company, journalists, at No. 1420 New York Avenue, where all the reporters can see them. I am going to the jail. CHARLES GUITEAU."

Like most disturbed people, Guiteau thrived on the attention he was receiving for his deed, and he penned a letter to what he termed "the Chicago Press" announcing that he was writing and would soon publish his autobiography, which would be called *The Life and Theology of Charles Guiteau*. He planned to use the money he made from this book to make bail, after which he could then go on a speaking tour similar to the ones he had done in the past. He assumed that his popularity would now be such that he would make enough money from these tours to hire the best lawyers to defend him and thus be acquitted of the charges brought against him.

Unfortunately for Guiteau, his jailers soon learned of his joy in seeing his name in print and stopped allowing him access to newspapers. This caused the prisoner to become increasingly agitated as the summer wore on. His guards, hardly faring any better in the summer heat, also became more and more irritable, and one of them, William Mason, finally had enough. In a fit of rage, Mason pulled out his side arm and fired at Guiteau, but the bullet hit one of the prison bars instead of the assassin. When the public heard what he had done, the jail was deluged with donations for Mason and his family, but he was still court-martialed for his deed and sentenced to eight years in prison.

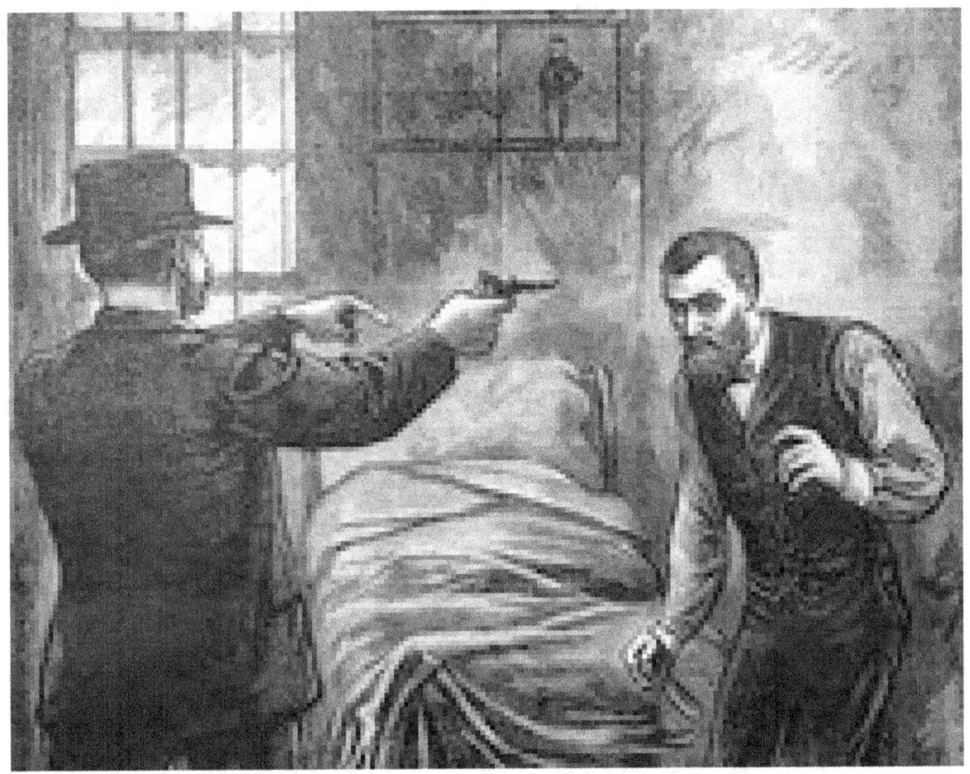

**An illustration depicting Mason's attempt to shoot Guiteau**

When he learned in September that Garfield had died, Guiteau collapsed and fell to his knees at the magnitude of the event, but he seemed to be back to normal (at least for him) by the following day. He even wrote to the new president, Chester Arthur, that Garfield's death "is a [godsend] to you & I presume you appreciate it. It raises you from $8,000 to $50,000 a year. It raises you from a political cypher to President of the United States with all its powers and honors…." After making some recommendations about cabinet positions, he concluded, "Let all honor be paid to Gen. Garfield's remains. He was a good man but a weak politician."

In October, Guiteau's autobiography, which he dictated from jail, was completed and published in the *New York Herald*, but perhaps not surprisingly, it did not bring him the sort of adulation he had expected as he continued to sit in jail. Meanwhile, George Corkhill, the district attorney who had been tasked with bringing him to justice, was busy preparing to prosecute the assassin. He knew Guiteau's defense attorney was likely to go with an insanity defense, and he would be ready for it.

On October 8, the prosecutor filed an indictment against Guiteau for Garfield's murder, and when Guiteau was arraigned six days later, George Scoville, Guiteau's brother-in-law, appeared on his behalf and was granted a continuance so that he could gather more evidence with which to make his case. Scoville hoped that the time he bought would allow him the ability to bolster the case that Guiteau was insane and that Garfield died as a result of poor medical care. In granting the continuance, Judge Walter Cox set the trial to begin the following month.

**Judge Cox**

**St. Elizabeth's Hospital, where Guiteau was housed during his trial**

By the time his trial began on November 14, 1881, Guiteau was in high spirits, anxious to be the center of the attention he so craved. He arrived a court dressed conservatively, in a black suit with a white shirt. When given the chance to speak, he asked only that nothing be done to offend "the Deity whose servant I was when I sought to remove the late President." Because of the notoriety of the case, the court found it difficult to find impartial jurors, and the final jury of 12 men included one African-American, a fact that Guiteau object to most strenuously.

From the very beginning, it was clear that Guiteau would not brook any attention falling on anyone other than himself. He began by insisting that he would not accept the representation of any "blunderbuss lawyers" and would instead make his own case, telling the court, "I came in here in the capacity as an agent of the Deity in this matter, and I am going to assert my right in this case."

For his part, Corkhill focused his attention on proving that Guiteau had indeed shot Garfield, and that the bullet had indeed ended the president's life. Dr. D. W. Bliss, who had performed the autopsy, made a most effective witness, using pieces of Garfield's actual vertebrae to demonstrate that the bullet Guiteau fired made the president's death inevitable, no matter how long it might have taken to happen. That afternoon, as Guiteau was being driven away from the courthouse, a drunken farmer named Bill Jones shot at him through the van bars but succeeded only in putting a hole in his coat.

When it came Scoville's turn, he tried to demonstrate to the jurors that his client was insane and should therefore receive treatment rather than punishment, telling them that such a move "is a change all the while progressing to a better state of things, to higher intelligence, to better judgment." However, while he was trying to make his case to the jury, Guiteau continued to interrupt him, repeatedly defending himself against Scoville's descriptions of his past behavior. Guiteau was willing to admit to being insane at the time of the shooting, but only because he believed that God had momentarily removed his free will and made him shoot Garfield, an interesting twist on the more traditional defense that the devil made him do it. Guiteau also believed that the doctors' negligence was primarily responsible for Garfield's death and questioned whether a court in Washington could try him given that the president died in New Jersey.

Scoville was almost certainly correct in determining that his best plan was to focus on the insanity angle, but Dr. John Gray, the superintendent of New York's Utica Asylum and the state's best witness, questioned Guiteau extensively before concluding that he had killed Garfield because of a sense of "wounded vanity and disappointment," not insanity. Then there was the matter of the M'Naghten rule, which required that in order to be found insane, the accused had to be unable to understand that what he did was against the law, and to know the possible consequences of his act. It was clear that Guiteau understood both that shooting Garfield was illegal and that the president might well die from his wounds. Indeed, he frequently testified that Garfield's death was his goal, and Guiteau also made it clear, in writing and on the stand, that he had carefully planned the shooting, so it was clearly not a crime of passion.

Still, Scoville was able to call a number of witnesses to testify of Guiteau's irrational behavior in the days before and after the shooting, and of course, no witness was as much anticipated as the accused himself, who took the stand on November 28, 1881. In the days that followed, first Scoville and then John Porter, a member of the prosecution, questioned him. In making his point that Guiteau did indeed know what he was doing, the latter led him through the plans he made in the days leading up to the shooting, leading Guiteau to testify, "I want it distinctly understood that I did not do that act in my own personality. I unite myself with the Deity, and I want you gentlemen to so understand it. I never should have shot the President on my own personal account. I want that distinctly understood. … The Deity furnished the money by which I bought [the pistol]. I was the agent of the Deity. … I have no objection to stating decidedly that I got $15 of Mr. Maynard's and used $10 of it to buy the pistol with. … It was of no consequence whether I got it from him or somebody else. Mr. Maynard did not know what I wanted the money for. I simply went to him and said, "I owe you $10 and I want to get $15 more, and I will give you a due-bill for the whole." He said to come in, in about fifteen minutes. It was then a quarter to 10 or such a matter, and I came in again and he gave me the money. That is all there is to it. It is of no consequence where I got the money or what I did with it. I do not claim that I was [inspired] to do the specific act; but I claim that the Deity inspired me to remove the President, and I had to use my ordinary judgment as to ways and means to accomplish the Deity's will. The inspiration consisted in trying to remove the President for the good of the American people, and all these details are nothing."

When asked about the ultimate outcome of his actions, Guiteau said, "The whole matter was in the hands of the Deity…. Of course, I appreciate the mere outward fact of the President's disability in his long sickness as much as any person in the world. That is a very narrow view to take of this matter--just the mere outward fact of the President's disability and sickness. I believed that it was the will of God that he should be removed, and that I was the appointed agent to do it."

Then there was the matter of whether or not he should be punished for his actions. On this point, Guiteau asserted, "If I had shot the President of the United States on my own personal account, no punishment would be too severe or too quick for me; but acting as the agent of the Deity puts an entirely different construction upon the act, and that is the thing that I want to put into this court and jury and the opposing counsel. I say this was an absolute necessity, in view of the political situation, for the good of the American people, and to save the nation from another war. That is the view I want you to entertain, and not settle down on a cold-blooded idea of murder. I never had the first conception of his removal as murder. I think the American people may sometime consider themselves under great obligations to me, sir."

At the same time, he maintained that he should not be punished for something over which he had no control: "After I got the conception, my mind was gradually being transformed and fixed as to the necessity of the act. My mind was not fully made up until about two weeks after--the two weeks I was resisting. I was finding out whether it was the Lord's will or not. Do you understand that? I was finding out whether it was God's will, and at the end I made up my mind that it was His will. That is the way I test the Lord. … I say that the Deity has confirmed the inspiration, thus far, and that He will take care of me. … Anything the Deity does is always right. He directed me to remove the President for the good of the American people. That is the way it always came to my mind. I never had any conception of it being a murder in the ordinary sense. I say the Deity killed the President, and not me. … I do not entertain the idea, sir, that there was any murder in this matter. There is no more murder in this matter than there would be to kill a man during the war. There was a homicide but no murder in it. I do not wish to discuss this matter with you any further, Judge Porter. It is altogether too sacred a matter for you to make light of, and I won't have it. You know my position on that point just as well as if you talked about it six weeks. It is too sacred to be discussed in this foolish, sickening kind of a way."

In spite of his rambling and often strange comments, the prosecution was able to get him to admit that there was much about his preparations for his deed that were obviously rational, including purchasing the pistol. Guiteau admitted, "I saw the pistol, and I noticed it the first time in a show-case. I saw a lot of pistols exposed for sale, and I saw this particular one, and I looked at it. … I am no expert on fire-arms at all, and never had a pistol before in my life, and knew nothing about using it. The man loaded it for me and I put it in my pocket. … I went out in the street. I do not know where I went with it." When he was questioned about why he knew to practice with the firearm before using it, Guiteau insisted, "I wanted to fire it off two or three times, as I knew nothing about a weapon, and I expected to be obliged to use it, and I wanted to familiarize myself with the outward uses of the weapon. I knew nothing about it, no more than a child."

This intrigued Parker and led to the following exchange:

"Q: You did not know how to shoot a pistol?

A: I knew nothing about it at all.

Q: But it was the Deity that was to shoot; didn't He know how?

A: There is no use of your whining in that kind of way; you may as well rest on that. You are making altogether too much talk about the mere outward act. I wish your mind to go back and look at the motive; the motive is what we are looking at.

Q: The motive was to kill, was it not?

A: To remove the President of the United States for the good of the American people, and the mere outward fact of how and when and where are all irrelevant matters. There is no use of your whining on this kind of talk any more."

Then there was the matter of his personal reasons for wanting the President dead, specifically that he had overlooked Guiteau in handing out jobs and that Guiteau hoped to use his new found notoriety to sell more books. The defendant admitted, "I should have removed the President any time from about the middle of June until I actually shot him if I had had an opportunity. …It was perfectly clear from the 1st of June, but I was not actually ready to do the act until about the middle of June. I had a good deal to do in the two weeks after the 1st of June until about the middle of June getting ready. For instance, I went to work and revised my book, The Truth. I knew there would be some demand for that. I also did several other matters, personal to myself, that I had to attend to; so, as a matter of fact, any time from the middle of June until the 2d of July if I had had an opportunity at the President, I should have shot him. I was watching for the opportunity during those two weeks. At any time during those two weeks I should have executed the divine will if I had had an opportunity…. I say that the entire responsibility of that thing is on the Deity; that He has taken care of it thus far, and that He will continue to take care of it. … The Deity uses certain men to serve Him. He is using this honorable court, and this jury, and all these policemen, and these troops to serve Him and to protect me."

**Guiteau on the witness stand.** *Harper's Weekly*

As far as the Deity's reasons for wanting Garfield dead, Guiteau insisted, "That was the misconduct of the President. He had gone back on Grant and Conkling and Arthur, the very men that carried New York, and without which he could not have been elected, and he then put himself right under the influence of Mr. Blaine."

Throughout his testimony, Guiteau repeatedly claimed that he did not see the dead president as a bad man, and that he in fact believe he was at that time in heaven: "No doubt he is a great deal happier now at this very moment than any man that is on earth. I presume he was a Christian man; I have no doubt of it at all. I think his Christian character had nothing whatever to do with his political record. Please put that down. His political record was, in my opinion, very poor; but his Christian character was good. Garfield was a good man, as far as I know, although they used to tell very hard stories about him on the Credit Mobilier business, and all that I don't know whether it was true or not. In my speech I defended him on that matter. Many papers were denouncing him as a thief and a Credit Mobilier rascal, and all that sort of thing, and we had fought very strongly against the attacks made upon him."

Of course, there was always the question in some people's minds as to whether or not some sort of conspiracy was afoot. While Guiteau denied any sort of understanding with Arthur about what he was going to do, he still wanted to point out his own importance: "I considered General Arthur my friend at that time, and do now. ...I was with him every day and night during the canvass in New York. ... I mean to say that when I went up to see General Arthur, I went right into his room. ...he had his private room, and only those who were supposed to be his personal friends were admitted. He had two or three rooms, and the crowd stayed back." Parker then asked him specifically, "You never had any conversation with him about murder, did you?" Guiteau replied, "No, sir; I did not. Neither he or General Grant knew anything about this inspiration."

Scoville's only hope to undo the damage done by Guiteau's own testimony was to bring in medical experts who could demonstrate that the man could not have known what he was doing when he shot the president. However, this proved to be a challenge. Dr. James Kienarn, a respected neurologist out of Chicago, explained to the jury that a man could indeed be insane without the accompanying delusions that were commonly believed to indicate mental disability. However, his testimony proved less than helpful once the prosecution got him to admit that he believed 20% or more of the population was either insane or one day would be. The defense called seven more doctors, but none of them seemed very effective.

Scoville had one last chance when he called a New York neurologist named Dr. Edward Spitzka to the stand. Spitzka testified extensively to Guiteau's obvious insanity until, under cross-examination, he was forced to admit that he was not actually a neurologist but instead a veterinarian. Almost 20 years later, Spitzka would participate in the autopsy of Leon Czolgosz, the anarchist who assassinated President William McKinley in September 1901.

EDWARD CHARLES SPITZKA, M.D.

PHYSICIAN AND BIOLOGIST

ALIENIST. WRITER ON MENTAL AND SPINAL DISEASES

### Spitzka

In response to the defense's now thoroughly trounced witnesses, the prosecution introduced Dr. Fordyce Barker, who told the court "there was no such disease in science as hereditary insanity" and that those who could not control themselves were in the throes of vice, not insanity. Dr. Noble Young, the prison's own physician, told the jury the Guiteau was not only "perfectly sane" but also "as bright and intelligent a man as you will ever see in a summer's day." Finally, Gray took the stand and made it clear that, following two days of interviewing Guiteau, he was certain that Guiteau, while depraved, was also sane.

Finally, on January 15, 1882, Guiteau got his chance to speak directly to the jury. He began, "I am going to sit down, because I can talk. I am not afraid of anyone shooting me.  This shooting business is declining. I am not here as a wicked man, or as a lunatic, I am here as a patriot and my speech is as follows.  I read from the New York Herald, gentlemen. It was sent by telegraph Sunday, and published in all the leading papers in America Monday. If the court please, gentlemen of the jury: I am a patriot. Today I suffer in bonds as a patriot. Washington was a patriot. Grant was a patriot. Washington led the armies of the Revolution through eight years of bloody war to victory and glory.  Grant led the armies of the Union to victory and glory, and today the nation is prosperous and happy.  They raised the old way-cry, 'Rally round the flag, boys,' and thousands of the choicest sons of the Republic went forth to battle, to victory or death. Washington and Grant, by their valor and success in war, won the admiration of mankind. Today I suffer in bonds as a patriot, because I had the inspiration and nerve to unite a great political party, to the end that the nation might be saved another desolating war.  In the grief and mourning that followed President Garfield's death, all contention ceased..."

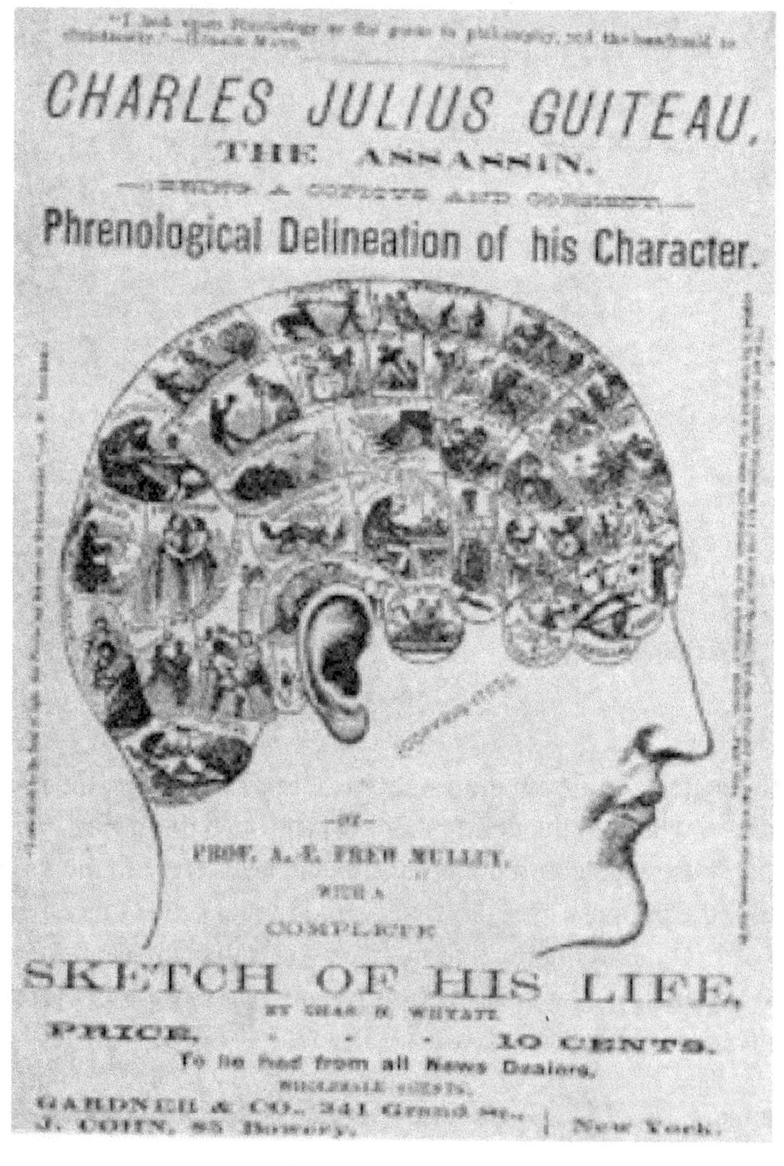

## A brochure published about Guiteau during his trial

He then reviewed his earlier statements while he had testified, namely that he did nothing to Garfield out of anger or malice, and that ultimately the president died due to the poor treatment he received from his doctors. While this is now obviously true, no one at that time could have known that with any certainty, and of course, had he not shot Garfield in the first place, the president would not have died.

Guiteau also brought up the issue of political disagreements in the United States, and his belief that with Garfield gone, these would be rectified. He even went so far as to read aloud "fan mail" that had been sent to him thanking him for his deed. He then returned to his topic, saying, "As sure as you are alive, gentlemen, as sure as you are alive, if a hair of my head is harmed this nation will go down to desolation... all you can do is put my body in the ground, but this nation will pay for it as sure as you are alive.  To hang a man in my mental condition on July 2 would be a lasting disgrace to the American people; they did not want the Republican party's savior hung. The mothers and daughters of the republic are praying that your will vindicate my inspiration, and their prayers I expect will prevail. A woman's instinct is keener than man's, and I pray you listen to the prayers of these ladies."

10 days later, when Judge Cox gave his charge to the jury, he made his feelings about Guiteau's ramblings very clear: "Before proceeding, I wish to interject here a remark upon an episode in the trial pending the last argument. The prisoner has taken repeated occasions to proclaim that public opinion, as evidenced by the press and by his correspondence, is in his favor. As you well know, these declarations could not have been prevented except by resorting to the process of gagging him. Any suggestion that you could be influenced by this lawless babble of the prisoner, would have seemed to me simply absurd, and I should have felt that I had almost insulted your intelligence if I had warned you not to regard it. The counsel for the prosecution have been rebuked for allowing these declarations to go to you without contradiction, and in the course of the final argument they felt it necessary to interpose a contradiction to these declarations of the prisoner, and the latter's counsel excepted to the form in which the contradiction was made. For the sole purpose of purging this record of any apparently objectionable matter, I would simply say, here, that nothing that has been said in reference to public sentiment or newspaper opinion, on either side, is to be regarded by you, although I really feel that such an admonition from me is totally unnecessary."

The judge then talked extensively about the need for proof and other factors they were to consider, finally handing them the case as the sun was setting on January 25, 1882. In just over an hour, the jury was back and the foreman, John P. Hamlin, announced that they had found Guiteau guilty. Upon hearing that, Guiteau cried out, "My blood be on the head of that jury; don't you forget it. That is my answer…God will avenge this outrage." When Cox sentenced him "to be hanged by the neck until you are dead," Guiteau replied, "I had rather stand where I am than where the jury does or where your Honor does."

**Judge Cox and the jury**

By the end of May, Guiteau had exhausted all his appeals, and a month later, on June 22, President Arthur heard his plea for a stay of execution but refused it. Guiteau complained, "Arthur has sealed his own doom and the doom of this nation."

For Guiteau, the day of his execution offered him the chance to give a final performance, and he was determined to make the most of his last moment in the spotlight. Mounting the gallows on June 30, 1882, he danced his way up to the scaffolding and then read 14 Bible verses. After that, he concluded with a poem he had composed for the occasion:

"I am going to the Lordy, I am so glad, I am going to the Lordy, I am so glad,
I am going to the Lordy, Glory hallelujah! Glory hallelujah!
I am going to the Lordy. I love the Lordy with all my soul, Glory hallelujah!
And that is the reason I am going to the Lord, Glory hallelujah! Glory hallelujah!
I am going to the Lord. I saved my party and my land, Glory hallelujah!
But they have murdered me for it, And that is the reason

"I am going to the Lordy, Glory hallelujah! Glory hallelujah!
I am going to the Lordy! I wonder what I will do when I get to the Lordy,
I guess that I will weep no more When I get to the Lordy! Glory hallelujah!
I wonder what I will see when I get to the Lordy, I expect to see most glorious things,
Beyond all earthly conception When I am with the Lordy! Glory hallelujah! Glory hallelujah!
I am with the Lord."

As these last words were spoken, the executioner pulled the lever and Guiteau fell, putting an end to one of the most tragic episodes in American history.

**Online Resources**

Other 19<sup>th</sup> century history titles by Charles River Editors

Other titles about James Garfield on Amazon

**Bibliography**

Ackerman, Kenneth D. (2003). Dark Horse: The Surprise Election and Political Murder of James A. Garfield. New York, New York: Avalon Publishing. ISBN 978-0-7867-1396-7.

Bach, Penny Balkin (1992). Public Art in Philadelphia. Philadelphia, Pennsylvania: Temple University Press. ISBN 978-0-87722-822-6.

Brown, Emma Elizabeth (1881). The Life and Public Services of James A. Garfield / Twentieth President of the United States. Boston, Massachusetts: D. Lothrop Company. OCLC 3037198.

Caldwell, Robert Granville (1965) [1931]. James A. Garfield: Party Chieftain. New York, New York: Dodd, Mead & Co. OCLC 833793627.

Clancy, Herbert J. (1958). The Presidential Election of 1880. Chicago, Illinois: Loyola University Press. ISBN 978-1-258-19190-0.

Crapol, Edward P. (2000). James G. Blaine: Architect of Empire. Biographies in American Foreign Policy. 4. Wilmington, Delaware: Scholarly Resources. ISBN 978-0-8420-2604-8.

Doenecke, Justus D. (1981). The Presidencies of James A. Garfield & Chester A. Arthur. Lawrence, Kansas: The Regents Press of Kansas. ISBN 978-0-7006-0208-7.

Garfield National Memorial Association (1890). The Man and the Mausoleum. Cleveland, Ohio: Cleveland Print and Publishing Company. OCLC 1656783.

McAlister, Lester G.; Tucker, William E. (1975). Journey in Faith: A History of the Christian Church (Disciples of Christ). St. Louis, Missouri: Chalice Press. ISBN 978-0-8272-1703-4.

McFeely, William S. (1981). Grant: A Biography. New York, New York: W. W. Norton & Company, Inc. ISBN 978-0-393-32394-8.

Peskin, Allan (1978). Garfield: A Biography. Kent, Ohio: Kent State University Press. ISBN 978-0-87338-210-6.

Radford, Warren; Radford, Georgia (2002). Outdoor Sculpture in San Francisco: a Heritage of Public Art. Gualala, California: Helsham Press. ISBN 978-0-9717607-1-4.

Rutkow, Ira (2006). James A. Garfield. New York, New York: Macmillan Publishers. ISBN 978-0-8050-6950-1. OCLC 255885600.

Smith, Jean Edward (2001). Grant. New York, New York: Simon & Schuster Paperback. ISBN 978-0-684-84927-0.

## Free Books by Charles River Editors

We have brand new titles available for free most days of the week. To see which of our titles are currently free, click on this link.

# Discounted Books by Charles River Editors

We have titles at a discount price of just 99 cents everyday. To see which of our titles are currently 99 cents, click on this link.

9 798627 165752